DECENTRALISED PAY SETTING

Decentralised Pay Setting

A Study of the Outcomes of Collective Bargaining Reform in the Civil Service in Australia, Sweden and the UK

K.A. BENDER

University of Wisconsin-Milwaukee

and

R.F. ELLIOTT

University of Aberdeen

Routledge
Taylor & Francis Group

LONDON AND NEW YORK

First published 2003 by Ashgate Publishing

Reissued 2018 by Routledge
2 Park Square, Milton Park, Abingdon, Oxon OX14 4RN
711 Third Avenue, New York, NY 10017, USA

Routledge is an imprint of the Taylor & Francis Group, an informa business

Publisher's Note
The publisher has gone to great lengths to ensure the quality of this reprint but points out that some imperfections in the original copies may be apparent.

Disclaimer
The publisher has made every effort to trace copyright holders and welcomes correspondence from those they have been unable to contact.

A Library of Congress record exists under LC control number: 2003043038

ISBN 13: 978-1-138-71571-4 (hbk)
ISBN 13: 978-1-315-19740-1 (ebk)

Contents

List of Figures, Tables and Appendices

Figures

Tables

Appendices

Acknowledgements

This book is the cumulation of research funded under a Leverhulme Trust grant between 1995-1997. The Trust's financial support for this research is gratefully acknowledged. In addition, we would like to thank the following people for their very helpful comments and considerable assistance in helping us to access the Civil Service pay records used in this study.

In Australia, we extend our thanks to Bernie Yates and all his colleagues in the Australian Department of Industrial Relations, and to Steven Jones of the National Office of the Community and Public Sector Union. All offered extremely helpful comments and engaged in discussions on public sector pay reform in Australian central government during the early 1990s. We are particularly grateful to Paul Nelson of the Public Service and Merit Protection Commission for his help in analysing the Australian Public Service Data.

In Sweden, conversations with Dr. Nils Henrik Schager of the National Agency of Government Employers (SAV) and Dr. Patrik Andersson were extremely helpful. They also assisted us in collecting information on public sector pay reform in Sweden. Patrik also supplied much useful information and guidance in analysing the Swedish Civil Service pay records. Johan Tengblad and Lena Moberg-Lindwall of the Union of Civil Servants also offered useful comment on this project.

Finally we wish to thank Nigel Barker and Bill Boulter of the Personnel Management and Conditions of Service Division of the UK Cabinet Office for their help in accessing the UK Mandate data.

We are also grateful to several people at the University of Aberdeen for their hard work in helping to complete this book. Samantha Ward greatly helped with tabulating some of the results from the data analysis of the Civil Service pay records. Ms Yat Wong and Anne Shipley typed early drafts of the manuscript. Lastly, we wish to extend particular thanks to Ms Sharron Smith for her hard work in preparing the final drafts of the book.

The dedication and conscientiousness of all the above have helped make this book possible.

Introduction

The 1990s witnessed profound changes in the way that many advanced industrialised countries paid their public sector workers. Confronted by pressures to contain public expenditure and improve the quality of public services, these countries introduced major public sector management reforms. These reforms had three principal elements; first, changes in financial management practices, second, reform of organisational structures and finally, the introduction of new personnel and reward systems. The reform of these first two elements necessarily preceded personnel and reward reform, but the three are inextricably linked. Without the final reform, the gains from the first two cannot be fully realised. Among the several different dimensions of the reform of personnel and reward systems the most important element is the reform of public sector pay systems. The purpose of the public management reforms was to improve public sector performance and efficiency: delivering improved services at lower cost. The single largest item of public sector current expenditure in all advanced industrial countries was, and remains, pay. Pay is also the principal motivator of those delivering the services. Its pivotal role in the reform process is therefore evident.

The most radical among the several forms of public management reform[1] introduced at this time was the move in some countries toward decentralised administrative structures and the subsequent decentralisation of pay systems.[2] Decentralised pay setting results in bargaining over pay and conditions of service at the level of separate government departments and agencies. The decision over pay and grading which were previously taken at a national level are now devolved to the separate administrative units. This happened in central government administration in Finland, New Zealand, Sweden and the UK and in the federal administration in Australia. Three of these five countries are the focus of this book.

This book analyses the impact of the decentralisation of the systems of pay setting in central government on the structures, level and growth of pay of civil servants in Australia Sweden and the UK. In so doing, it provides the most detailed analysis of the pay of civil servants in these three countries that is available.

---

[1] For a very detailed and informative discussion of public management reform see Pollitt and Bouckaert (2000).

[2] Of course, administrative decentralisation is not the only form that the move to decentralisation assumed during the nineteen nineties. Some countries also introduced political decentralisation at this time and indeed political decentralisation remains a very live issue at the start of the 21st Century. However, it was not the cause of the reform of pay systems in central government in the three countries studied here which is the focus of this book.

The appeal of decentralised systems has been well described by Pollitt and Bouckaert (2000), who remark that 'Decentralisation, ministers and mandarins have said, makes possible more responsive and speedy public services, better attuned to local and/or individual needs. It facilitates 'downsizing' by leading to elimination of unnecessary layers of middle management. It even produces more contented and stimulated staff, whose jobs have been 'enriched' by taking on devolved responsibilities for financial and personnel management, and by escaping from the overburden of centralised regulation' (op. cit p83).

The counterpart of these advantages of decentralised administrative systems is that of decentralisation of pay systems. As we shall detail in the first chapter, this makes possible pay and reward structures that are attuned to the employing organisation's goals. It makes possible pay structures that are attuned to the labour markets in which the employing organisation operates and it enables the construction of pay systems that will motivate employee performance to meet organisational goals. Decentralisation of pay setting might thus be expected to have a profound impact on the way civil servants are paid and to change fundamentally the structure of rewards.

In this book we analyse the outcomes of these reforms. We seek to identify the initial impact that these reforms have had on the structure of pay in central government in three countries. We look at the impact of decentralisation on the pay of civil servants in these three countries and identify the effect that decentralisation had on the inequality of pay both within departments, agencies and ministries, and between different departments, agencies and ministries. We identify the differences in the rates of pay growth for the different grades of civil servants that lie behind the changes in pay inequality and we seek to identify whether decentralisation changed the way in which civil servants are paid. We examine if reform has changed the way in which the skills of civil servants are rewarded for it is likely that some civil servants have benefited more from decentralisation than others. We seek to distinguish who the gainers and losers are. These are just some of the questions addressed in this book.

We focus on the experience of Australia, Sweden and the UK because the nature and origins of administrative decentralisation and pay setting differed between them. Moreover, the labour markets in which the public sector operated differed in these three countries since the wage structure in the private sector, with whom the civil service compete for labour, was different in these countries. As a result, we expect the impact of the reforms of pay structure to vary between these three countries. These differences are detailed and explored fully in the subsequent chapters.

The first chapter details the theoretical arguments for decentralised pay setting arrangements. It identifies both the advantages and the disadvantages of a decentralised system. It is followed by a chapter detailing the nature of the data we use in our empirical work, and explaining how we have processed this data and the variables we have created. It also outlines the basic empirical methods we employ in the subsequent analysis. This second chapter is followed by three country chapters, where each is devoted to the detailed analysis of the form of public and private sector wage setting, the nature and motivation for the reform of pay setting and the impact that this has had on pay and pay structure in each of these countries. A sixth chapter contrasts the experience of the three countries, identifying and explaining differences in the observed outcomes in the three countries.

References

Pollitt, C. and Bouckaert, G. (2000) *Public Management Reform: A Comparative Analysis*, Oxford, Oxford University Press.

Chapter 1

The Theoretical Arguments for Decentralised Pay Setting Arrangements

Introduction

One of the major determinants of the drive to decentralise the systems for setting the pay of public sector workers in Australia, Sweden and the UK during the nineteen nineties was developments in the private sector of the economies of these three countries. A very limited theoretical literature has analysed the determinants of the institutional arrangements for pay setting in the private sector of industrialised economies. There has been some analysis of the impact of collective bargaining on economic performance but this has taken collective bargaining arrangements as exogenous even though it has been recognised that these arrangements have changed through time. There has been virtually no discussion of the determinants of pay setting arrangements in the public sector and more specifically of the determinants of decentralisation in the non-market, public sector of these industrialised economies.[1] Beyond the familiar debate about the association between bargaining structure and macroeconomic performance (see Calmfors and Driffel, 1988, Soskice, 1990 and Flanagan, 1999) there has been no detailed analysis of the relative advantages and disadvantages of centralised and decentralised bargaining arrangements, at the microeconomic level in either the public or private sectors. The focus of this chapter is therefore upon a more detailed theoretical analysis of the determinants of and advantages and disadvantages of decentralised wage setting in the public sector.

The Chapter begins with a detailed analysis of the reasons for the reform of private sector wage structures. It highlights the changing nature of product markets and the consequences of this for the institutions of pay setting and the resulting growth of pay inequality in some countries. This growth in private sector pay inequality had a profound impact on the labour markets in which the public sector operates. In some countries this development together with the perceived advantages of decentralised system of pay setting in the private sector persuaded governments to seek similar reforms to public sector pay setting. The chapter therefore continues with a detailed analysis of the perceived advantages of decentralised systems of pay setting in first the private and then the public sector. Finally it records some of the disadvantages of decentralised systems which may help explain why not all industrialised countries have chosen this path of reform.

---

[1] Perhaps the single exception is the Macroeconomic perspective offered by Eichengreen and Iversen (1999).

Decentralisation in the Private Sector

The reform of the system for setting pay in the private sector of the economy in two of the three countries studied here, Sweden and the UK, preceded the moves to decentralise bargaining arrangements in the public sector. In Australia the changes happened at the same time in the two sectors. Developments in the labour markets in which the private sector operates will have significant repercussions on public sector labour markets, and therefore the reform of private sector pay setting acted as a powerful incentive to reform the public sector labour markets in these countries. It is therefore important to understand the reasons for the reform of pay bargaining in the private sector although it should be understood that the reforms in the public sector were not just a response to the reforms in private sector labour markets. There are several additional reasons, outlined below, to explain why governments saw fit to reform bargaining arrangements in the public sector. Before we discuss these, we examine the reasons for the move to decentralisation in the private sector of these economies. We shall discuss the timing and specific nature of the move to decentralisation in each country in more detail in the country specific chapters.

The Determinants of Private Sector Decentralisation

There is a substantial microeconomic literature on models of wage determination. Some of this has involved a discussion of union and employer preferences for and the employment and inflation consequences of, different bargaining structures. From this literature can be distinguished a number of reasons for the decentralisation of bargaining in the private sector. They are as follows.

Drive to reduce costs in response to intensified competition in product markets The critical development seems to have been a fundamental change in the nature of the product markets in which private sector firms operate. Product markets have broadened as the barriers to international trade have been dismantled while the quickening pace of technological change has meant that the entry of new firms has become easier. Both these developments have resulted in intensified competition in product markets. This intensified competition has served to undermine union power which arises from the unions' ability to co-ordinate wage and employment policy over the whole of the relevant product market (see Flanagan, 1999, p. 1170). Intensified competition has made this less possible. These same developments have also reduced the economic rents available to employers and employees alike and have threatened the existence of less efficient producers.

One consequence of the intensified competition has been an intensified drive to reduce costs. This has diminished firms' enthusiasm for those arrangements that previously served to mitigate the degree of competition among domestic producers. One such arrangement was centralised wage agreements which set a floor under wage costs and had the effect of 'taking wages out of competition'. The drive to reduce costs also led to an intensified search for further improvements in labour productivity in order to reduce unit labour costs. Firms sought improvements in labour productivity by seeking to improve employee motivation. Introducing new pay structures and reward systems has been seen as one method of achieving this. The importance of local bargaining in providing a reward for greater effort on the job has been revealed in models of union wage bargaining in which local bargaining can be viewed as a form of profit sharing (Moene *et al.* 1993).

Decentralised corporate structures resulting from increasing product heterogeneity A second fundamental change in the nature of product markets has been increasing product heterogeneity. Firms have been confronted by an increasing diversity and sophistication of consumers tastes, and they have also sought to create greater product diversity as a means of securing temporary monopoly advantage in order to raise profitability.[2] Again the consequence for labour markets is that these developments result in firm specific pressures to contain or adjust costs which in turn encourages firms to create their own pay and grading structures for these will offer more direct control of costs.

The shift from mass production to more diversified skill based methods of production together with the emergence of greater volatility and uncertainty in the economic environment (Piore and Sabel, 1984) has resulted in a movement toward decentralised corporate structures. In some industries decentralisation *within* corporations has occurred as the firm is split into separate profit centres, while in others the forces identified above have principally resulted in substantially greater diversity in organisational structure *between* corporations. The decentralisation of corporate structures has resulted in pressures to end the old centralised bargaining arrangements. Decentralised bargaining can be viewed as an essential counterpart to decentralised organisational structures.

One advantage of decentralised organisational structures and hence decentralised decision making is that it produces greater efficiency in information flows, resulting in greater efficiency in the transmission of information about 'time and place'. In a firm, this means information about production processes and markets which potentially, makes the firm more flexible in meeting the demands of the market. Such information, it has been argued, cannot be centralised without losing or distorting much of the content of the information.

Increasing pace of technological change and diversity Underpinning the changes in the nature of product markets have been changes in technology and the pace of technological-change. The product life-cycle appears to be shortening, with the result that production technologies and their associated labour skills are changing more rapidly. A consequence of greater product heterogeneity is greater diversity of technology and a greater diversity and often specificity of skills at the company level. Eichengreen and Iversen (1999) have emphasised the increased heterogeneity of labour that accompanied the decline of the dominant Fordist

---

[2] Suen (1991) shows that consumers value product diversity and are willing to pay more for heterogeneous products, while Kahn (1998) offers theories of the advantages to businesses in offering differentiated products.

model of production. Companies have as a result constructed pay and grading structures, which are appropriate to their specific skill mix and which encourage the appropriate employment and redeployment of labour.

Weakened Trade Unions

The above developments in product markets have had substantial repercussions for labour markets. The changing characteristics of product markets have eroded unions ability to co-ordinate wage and employment over an entire product market. Firms have resisted co-ordination and sought to decentralise pay setting. In the UK these developments have lead to a weakening of the collective bargaining power of unions, which has been reinforced by changes in the legislative framework that had earlier protected union power. This latter is a reflection of the weakened political power of trade unions.

In all three countries, parties, primarily of the political right, without links to trade unions gained power during the nineteen eighties, and as public opinion moved against trade unions,[3] unions began to change their policies and to lower their resistance to decentralised bargaining arrangements. It is difficult to find robust data to support the statement that union power weakened substantially during the 1980s and early 1990s but some evidence is provided in the following tables.

The most frequently documented element is the decline in union membership. Among the three countries studied here, this decline was greatest in the UK[4] over the period from 1970 to the middle 1990s (see Table 1.1).

Table 1.1 Trade Union Density*

	1970	1980	1990	1996/7
Australia	50.2 (1976)	48.0 (1982)	40.4	34.7 (1996)
Sweden	67.7	79.7	82.5	87.7 (1997)
UK	44.8	50.4	39.1	33.4 (1997)

Note: Trade Union membership as percentage of employed wage and salary earners.

Source: OECD, *Employment Outlook*, July 1994, and Labour Force Statistics

---

[3] Though there is some debate over the effect of public opinion on trade unions, Walsh (1988), Marsh *et al* (1990), and Jarley and Kuruvilla (1994) all find that public opinion is negatively influenced by at least some union activities such as strikes.

[4] Overall figures on union density, which are those most generally available, mask the scale of the decline in the private sector because union membership has held up in the public sector in most countries.

Union membership is, however, only one indicator of the change in collective bargaining power that has occurred, another is the coverage of collective agreements. Not all union members have their pay set by collective bargaining for there may be too few of them in the firm. On the other hand, some non-union workers may have their pay set through collective bargaining because the firm extends union negotiated terms and conditions to all its employees, regardless of whether they are union members or not. The difference between union membership and coverage (see Tables 1.1 and 1.2) is much less in Sweden, than in either the UK or Australia. In the UK, trade union density stood at 50 per cent in 1980 while coverage extended to 70 per cent of employees. In Australia, in the same year, membership stood at around 48 per cent and coverage was 88 per cent. Table 1.2 indicates that coverage fell sharply in the UK between 1980 and 1994 but declined only slightly in Australia while it was virtually unchanged in Sweden. Table 1.2 also reveals the substantial difference between collective bargaining coverage in the public and private sectors in all three countries in 1990. In all three, coverage was much higher in the public sector than it was in the private sector.

Table 1.2 Collective Bargaining Coverage between 1980 and 1994

	Collective Bargaining Coverage		Collective Bargaining Coverage in 1990		
	1980	1994	Overall	Public	Private
Australia	88	80	80	98	72
Sweden	86	89	83	100	72
UK	70	47	47	78	40

Source: OECD, *Employment Outlook*, July 1994 and Flanagan (1999)

There has been much empirical work into the causes of the decline in union density. (See Carruth and Disney, 1988, for an example for the UK). Any significant reduction in trade union density and perhaps collective bargaining coverage, is likely to reduce trade unions capacity to resist the reform of pay setting arrangements and in particular their capacity to resist attempts to decentralise bargaining arrangements.

Perhaps a further indication of the decline in unions will or perhaps power to resist change is the fall in strike activity that has occurred in all three countries over the period from the mid 1980s to the mid 1990s. This has been of quite substantial proportions as Table 1.3 shows. Still, other changes have been the weakened political power of labour interest groups as a result of the election of right of centre governments and the subsequent change in policies in response to this on the part of unions.

Table 1.3 Average Number of Working Days Lost per 1000 Employees Due to Strike Action in Selected Industries*

	1985-89	1990-94	1995-99
Australia	524	377	89
Sweden	120	44	45
UK	380	69	21

Note: Mining and quarrying, Manufacturing, Construction, Transport and Communications.
Source: Department of Education and Employment, *Labour Market Trends*, June 1996 and April 2001.

The reduction in the power of unions and in particular in their capacity to resist change, makes it easier for management to shift the locus of bargaining to achieve more favourable outcomes. This shift in bargaining power may have been a necessary condition for decentralisation in the UK. The reduction in union power has been greatest in the UK, while, save for the reductions in strike activity, there has been less change in Australia and Sweden. However, more important than the reduction in union power was the dramatic changes in product markets and technology which provided the motivation for decentralisation in all three countries. As the country specific chapters will show decentralised pay setting exists in the private sector in all three countries.

The Consequences of Decentralised Pay Setting in the Private Sector

The changes in wage setting arrangements in the private sector had significant effects on pay outcomes in that sector. They resulted in changes in pay structure in the private sector which had dramatic effects on the labour markets in which public sector employers operated. There were two important dimensions to these changes in the private sector.

Variations in the size of pay settlements and in rates of pay The move from national or industry bargaining to decentralised pay setting resulted in many more separate bargaining and pay setting units. Each of these struck a bargain reflecting the particular preferences and perceived opportunities of the unions and employers in each unit and there was therefore much greater variation in the size of pay settlements and rates of pay than under centralised arrangements. The variation in pay is likely to be greatest where it is the employer who unilaterally determines the rates of pay (Jackson *et al.*, 1993, and Dowrick, 1993). However, there will still be diversity where pay is set by collective bargaining, because of variations in union power, and differences in the local labour market in which firms operate. There may also be differences in the amount of economic rent to be distributed, due to differences in the product markets in which firms operate, the technologies they employ and company productivity. We should therefore expect to observe substantial changes in pay structure as a result of decentralisation emerging after a number of years. Just how large the change will be will depend on the pace and extent of change.

Increased pay dispersion   It has been shown that the more decentralised a country's wage setting arrangements, the more dispersed is pay. It has been shown that pay dispersion is negatively correlated with the degree of centralisation of collective bargaining (OECD, 1997). Flanagan (1999) has argued that many centralised bargaining systems seem to award relatively large pay increases to the lowest paid union members while restraining the wage gains of the most highly skilled although 'distinguishing the relative effects of market and institutional influences on wage inequality can be more of an art than a science' (p1163). However, it has also been shown that during the 1980s and 1990s wage inequality grew least in those countries with centralised bargaining arrangements (Gottschalk and Smeeding, 1997) and most in countries with decentralised bargaining arrangements (OECD, 1997). Country specific evidence for Sweden, Norway and New Zealand reveals that the move to more decentralised arrangements in the private sector of these countries was associated with increased pay dispersion.

These developments in the private sector exerted a powerful influence for change in the public sector. There are additional reasons to seek the reform of pay setting arrangements in the public sector which we review below. Yet the absence of the market pressures that confront the private sector means that the outcome in the public sector may not be the same as that in the private sector.

Table 1.4 Trend in Earnings Dispersions (All Employees)

	1980	1985	1990	1995
Australia				
9th Decile/1st Decile	2.79	2.72	2.81	2.90
9th Decile/Median	1.70	1.66	1.66	1.77
1st Decile/Median	0.61	0.61	0.59	0.61
Sweden				
9th Decile/1st Decile	2.04	2.06	2.00	2.12*
9th Decile/Median	1.57	1.59	1.52	1.59
1st Decile/Median	0.77	0.77	0.76	0.75
United Kingdom				
9th Decile/1st Decile	2.78	3.05	3.28	3.40
9th Decile/Median	1.67	1.77	1.84	1.87
1st Decile/Median	0.60	0.58	0.56	0.55

Note: Data for Sweden for 1995 was not available, hence data for 1993 has been used

Source: OECD *Employment Outlook*, June 1996

Table 1.4 reports data on earnings dispersions in Australia, Sweden and the UK over the period from 1980 to the mid 1990s. One problem with this data is that it is not available for the private sector only, hence developments in the public sector will mask changes in the private sector. This said, there does appear to be a sharp widening of earnings dispersion in the UK over the period 1980–1990 as private sector decentralisation proceeded, while in Sweden earnings dispersion appears to be widening after 1990. The process that produced this widening is depicted in Figure 1.1 below.

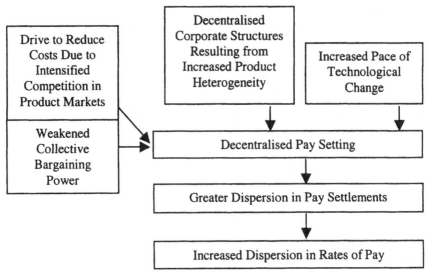

Figure 1.1 The Process Resulting in Increased Pay Inequality

Arguments for Public Sector Pay Setting Reform[5]

The decentralisation of pay bargaining in the private sector had a significant impact on the public sector for it changed many of the labour markets in which the public sector operates. Moreover, politicians believed that private sector decentralisation was motivated by efficiency concerns and they wanted to change the system of pay setting in the public sector in order to introduce similar disciplines and to improve efficiency. However, these were not only motivations for public sector pay setting reform. There were other more general influences, not experienced by firms in the private sector, which motivated the public sector reforms. This next section identifies the three most important general reasons given for reforming the way public sector pay is set, while in the section following the reasons why this reform took the form of decentralisation are detailed.

---

[5] This section details the general pressures for reforming public sector pay in the three countries. See the individual country chapters for more detail on the specific pressures in each of the three countries.

Macroeconomic Pressures

During the nineteen nineties, most of the countries of the European Union sought to meet the Maastricht criteria for membership of the European Monetary Union. These criteria included, among others, ceilings on both the ratios of total government debt to GDP and the annual rate of government borrowing to GDP, each of which placed substantial constraints on the level of public expenditure. Although Sweden and the UK chose not to join in the first wave, there was also substantial pressure to reduce public expenditure in both these countries because in the early 1990s public debt was thought to be unsustainably high for that stage of the economic cycle. In Australia such motivations were absent but control over public spending was still seen as a macroeconomic priority.

The public sector pay bill is the single largest element of government current expenditure and thus any attempt to contain or reduce government expenditure is likely to result in attempts to constrain public sector pay growth. One of the motivations for reform in all three countries was the idea that the reform of pay structures might allow better control of one major element of public expenditure: the public sector pay bill.

Organisational Reform

A second motivation for reform was the move to reform the organisations that deliver public services. The services produced by the public sector are many and diverse and in some countries it was thought that the organisational structures which deliver these services should reflect this diversity. In all three countries studied here, but perhaps more so in the UK and Sweden, a distinction was made in central government between the core activities of making policy and the related activities of delivering the services resulting from these policies. The former was to be the responsibility of central government departments, while the latter would now be provided by separate agencies. The approach to the reform of central government that was adopted, sought to recognise this diversity and to allow those in charge of service delivery to 're-engineer' their organisations and ultimately to construct pay structures appropriate to the diversity of the services they provided.

Pay Structure

A final motivation was the perceived imbalance between the pay structures that existed in the public and private sectors. One dimension of this imbalance was that the minimum rates of pay for the least skilled occupations were believed to be higher in the public sector than the private. This was likely due to both the greater prominence of unions and the more effective use of union power in this sector, since unions tend to flatten the wage structure (Freeman, 1980 and Metcalf *et. al.*, 2000). Reinforcing this was the fact that in the past, the state sought to be seen as a good employer, offering 'fair' rates of pay to the least skilled. This tended to raise the rates paid to the least skilled in the public sector above those paid to similar workers in the private sector. A second dimension of this imbalance was that the rates paid to the most senior public servants were substantially less than those paid to individuals with comparable levels of skill and responsibility in the private sector. Public opposition to high rates of pay for public servants in part accounted for this feature (Katz and Krueger, 1993).

The combined effect of both of these last two features of the pay structure was a much flatter pay structure in the public sector than existed in the private sector (see Figure 1.2 below). The economic consequences of such an imbalance were that the public sector was paying more than it needed to attract, retain, and motivate unskilled and low skilled labour, thus, from an efficiency view it was wasting resources. On the other hand, the rates it paid to the most highly skilled or those with the greatest responsibilities were less than was needed to attract, retain, and motivate, which had adverse consequences for wastage rates and recruitment.

Thus there were powerful arguments for reforming public sector wage setting. However, it is conceivable that these reforms might have assumed a different form to decentralisation. What were the further set of arguments that resulted in the move to decentralisation? These are detailed in the following section.

Perceived Advantages of Decentralised Pay Setting in the Public Sector

Like the private sector, the introduction of decentralised pay setting arrangements in the public sector complements organisational and administrative decentralisation. Decentralised pay setting complements administrative decentralisation for it offers those changed with managing these decentralised organisations a number of quite distinct advantages over the previous more centralised pay structures.

Earnings

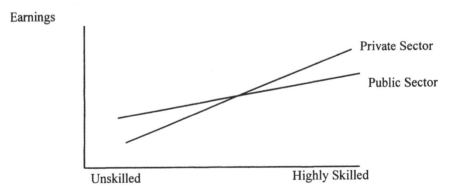

Figure 1.2 The 'Double Imbalance'

Realigning Pay

Decentralised pay setting allows public sector organisations to pay market rates. If the relevant labour market is the local labour market and the rates paid are out of line with that market, they can be brought more closely into line with those paid by other employees. If the organisation recruits its labour from a small number of local markets, there is no need to make reference to the wider national market. Delegation also offers the opportunity for organisations to adjust senior managerial rates upwards towards levels appropriate to the risks and responsibilities associated with senior jobs. Thus we should expect to see the pay structure widening as rates at the bottom fall or grow less rapidly and those at the top rise.

Heterogeneity of Public Services

The public sector in most advanced industries provides a very wide range of services to the public. These range from education to tax collection, from legal services to defence. The organisational forms appropriate for the delivery of these services vary greatly. Decentralised pay setting arrangements permit more diverse pay and grading structures; they permit structures which are more attuned to organisational goals and to the diverse services the organisations deliver. Under decentralised arrangements, departments and agencies that assume responsibility for pay and grading can introduce those most appropriate for their organisation. Where they adopt leaner and flatter organisational structures, like those which have grown in the private sector in recent years, reform of pay structures will be necessary.

Clarifying Organisational Goals

The assumption of delegated responsibility for pay and grading may also encourage management in public sector organisations to think more fundamentally about the objectives of the organisations they run. Charged with responsibility for redesigning the reward structure, or even confirming the appropriateness of the existing one, management must decide how the pay and reward structure helps meet the organisations' strategic objectives. In turn this may lead them to better define those organisations goals.

Encouraging Innovation

Government departments charged with responsibility for pay and grading may review the organisation of work. Managers may be encouraged to experiment with both the organisation of work and with different payment systems such as team and individual reward. Different methods of tying pay to performance and different mechanisms for pay enhancement may also be tried. Such experimentation is unlikely to be costless, mistakes will be made, but under a delegated systems the costs are likely to be organisation and not sector specific. Experimentation may help identify 'best practice', and when it is identified, it can be passed on to other parts of the public sector. Because public sector organisations are almost never in competition with one another the barriers that stand in the way of transfer of best practice in a competitive environment do not exist in the public sector. The encouragement of innovation in reward structures may be a major benefit of decentralisation.

Increased Investment in Training

The public sector employs a mix of general and specific skills. Under centralised pay structures, career paths and reward structures were usually service-wide and most training was either general or sector specific, almost never department specific. Employees were encouraged to develop skills that allowed them to move between departments and because employees moved between departments, often after relatively short periods in post, most government departments had little incentive to invest in training. Departments were reluctant to invest in skills, because they would have been unable to earn a return on the investment. Furthermore, employees, particularly those with the highest education levels, had no incentive to invest in department specific skills. For these employees the payoff to specific skills was lower than that to general skills because the rewards in the public sector did not match those in the private sector. The reform of pay structures and the emergence of pay, grading and career structures which are organisation specific will change this.

When they have responsibility for pay and grading structures, organisations can design structures that offer incentives to departments and individuals to invest in department specific skills. They can design reward systems that induce their employees to stay with the organisation for a period of time that is sufficient to allow both the organisation and the individual to earn a return on their share of the investment. The development of pay structures which reward long term commitment will encourage investment in specific skills.

Possible Disadvantages of Decentralised Pay Setting in the Public Sector

There are a number of disadvantages which need to be weighed against the above and which need to be understood when evaluating the case for decentralisation. For the most part these disadvantages result from important differences between the private and public sectors. If present to any substantial degree, they will dispose some public sector organisations toward a co-operative rather than a decentralised strategy for pay setting.

Reduced Co-operation

One important motivator of decentralised pay setting in the private sector was intensified competition in product markets. This would appear to have resulted in a reduction in the returns from co-operation among firms in the private sector. However, this pressure is not evident in the public sector and therefore public sector organisations may see advantages in cooperating to set pay. There are at least two reasons why they might wish to do so. First, if they co-operate they can exchange experience and information in order to improve the performance of the sector as a whole. Second, the transaction costs associated with setting pay can be reduced. The transaction costs associated with setting pay and posting salary schedules could be substantial under a decentralised system. Among these costs are the 'menu' costs, the costs of announcing new pay rates, and the costs associated with the process of pay bargaining. These costs will rise as the number of different bargaining units and associated salary schedules rises. A decentralised system replaces the single pay bargain of the centralised system with many separate negotiations, leading to substantially higher administrative and bargaining costs.

Opaque Wage Signals

Under a decentralised system each organisation constructs its own pay and grading structure and conducts its own pay negotiations, while in a centralised system, there is a single pay schedule and grading structure. Thus under a decentralised system, those individuals seeking work, changing jobs or merely monitoring developments in the market, will have to acquire and process a substantially greater amount of information than under a centralised system. One consequence of this greater amount of information is that decentralised systems present individuals with greater opportunities for making mistakes. They will also be associated with greater uncertainty over the true structure of relative rewards at times when the larger numbers of pay structures that will exist are subject to frequent change. Both these features could discourage employees from undertaking further investment in skills.

   Centralised systems in contrast offer the advantage that information about the relative structure of rewards is both more easily transmitted and assessed. Moreover, a single national pay and grading structure may assist inter-organisational and inter-regional staff re-deployment. Under a centralised system, staff may be offered the same rate of pay in several different jobs and regions of the country. If staff suffer from money illusion or are unsure about the pattern of real pay they may be more willing to switch jobs or to change the place they work under a centralised system than under a decentralised system.

Opportunities for Monopsonistic or Monopolistic Behaviour

A decentralised system might result in the exploitation of either monopsony or monopoly power. Where a public sector organisation is the sole buyer of a particular skill in a local market, opportunities for monopsonistic behaviour exist and pay may be driven down under decentralised pay setting. In contrast, where the employer is covered by centralised wage setting arrangements, these opportunities for monopsonistic behaviour at the local level are removed.

   Decentralisation could also expose the employer to the exploitation of monopolistic behaviour on the part of the union where the union is the sole 'seller' of labour in the local market. Under these circumstances, the union could seek to set the rate of pay at which employers can hire labour in the local market above the labour market clearing rate. The degree of competition for labour in the local market will determine which, if any, of these consequences of decentralisation emerge.

The Consequences of Decentralising Pay Bargaining for Wage Inflation

There is one final issue which is usually at the forefront of any discussion about the economic impact of decentralised pay setting and that is its impact on wage inflation. However, the literature on the effects of different bargaining arrangements on employment and inflation, contains no specific discussion of the public sector. The argument is framed purely in terms of profit maximising firms in the private sector. The reason for this omission is the obvious difficulty of specifying the public sector employer's objective function in the absence of profit maximising behaviour. In the absence of such behaviour it is difficult to map out the responses of the parties to changes in the objective conditions confronting the public organisation.

The literature on this topic proposes that there is a 'hump-shaped' relationship between the level of bargaining and wage inflation, with low wage inflation associated with either very centralised or completely decentralised systems of pay bargaining and high wage inflation associated with systems falling in between these two extremes (see Calmfors and Driffill, 1988, Soskice, 1990, Calmfors, 1993, and Flanagan, 1999). The economic concept of the derived demand for labour helps explain why these relationships emerge. This concept states that the demand for labour derives from the demand for the product that labour produces and one of the determinants of the elasticity of the demand for labour will therefore be the elasticity of final product demand. Even though the services that are produced by the public sector are most frequently provided free at the point of consumption this concept will still apply. This is because the services provided still involve the use of scarce resources, and so there is an opportunity cost and therefore an implicit cost of production. These costs have to be met out of taxes and therefore they have implicit prices.[6] The concept of the elasticity of demand for labour can therefore still apply to the public sector.

In the private sector it is argued that under centralised systems, unions which are nationally organised 'internalise the externalities' of the trade-off

---

[6] While it may seem strange to speak about a demand curve for public sector goods and services, many of which are not traded on a market, there are still prices at which these goods/services are offered. These implicit or shadow prices will be indirect taking the form of taxes or votes for the government in power (i.e. these services must be provided in order for the government to stay in power) and will reflect the value of these goods and services to society. The labour needed to supply these will then depend upon the demand for these goods and services at different levels of these implicit prices and will therefore be derived from it.

between pay and employment. At this aggregate level unions face a highly elastic demand curve for labour and because national unions care about both pay and employment on an economy-wide basis they moderate pay demands to ensure a minimal reduction in employment. At the other extreme, wage inflation in decentralised systems is also kept low, due to the absence of market power on the part of firms. The absence of market power is because there are many producers of most private sector goods and services. Under a decentralised system the firm is a separate bargaining unit and the absence of market power means that the union with which it bargains faces a very elastic demand curve for the labour it represents. If the union pushed for a large pay increase there would be a big reduction in employment. The elastic labour demand curve moderates pay growth in decentralised systems.

This framework has only limited application in the public sector because product markets are very different (Bender, 1998, and Gregory and Borland, 1999) and this can result in very different outcomes. Centralised bargaining will still limit pay growth in the public sector, due to the internalisation of the pay-employment trade-off as above but the case of decentralised bargaining is much different. In the private sector the derived demand for labour at the level of a single bargaining unit is likely to be highly elastic but in central government, agencies and departments are overwhelmingly monopoly producers of the services they provide. Because they are monopoly producers, demand is relatively inelastic at these implicit prices. The demand for labour in the agencies and departments of central government is therefore more inelastic than at the firm level in the private sector. The result is that the pay-employment trade-off is smaller for decentralised bargaining units in the public sector than for decentralised units in the private sector. Hence, all other things equal, decentralised pay bargaining in the public sector will result in higher pay settlements than under either centralised bargaining or decentralised private sector bargaining.[7]

Recognising the above, government might intervene more directly to try to change the elasticity of labour demand in the public sector. One method of achieving this is by imposing cash limits or frame grants. When the government successfully imposes cash limits there is unit elasticity and a one-to-one relationship between percentage changes in wages and employment. However, in many areas of government activity this approach is very difficult to sustain. This is because the government will not wish to see a severe decline in the output or the services of many agencies. It may well be more concerned about the global spending total than spending at the agency and department level. Under these circumstances it will be prepared to shuffle funds around within the global total

---

[7] Of course an important determinant of pay growth is the stance, power, and militancy of public sector unions. Unionism is very high in the public sector of all three countries, and though it is only an indirect measure of the power of unions, the potential for unions to take advantage of the inelastic labour demand curve is still an important factor in pay bargaining in all three countries.

and the labour demand curve could, in practice, be quite inelastic at the level of some departments and agencies.

Critical to the above line of argument is the assumption that both the employers' and the unions' objective functions contain employment and pay as arguments. This may not be correct, if the policy maker's only concern is to control the growth of the pay bill. Public sector employment will then be a very secondary concern.

However, policy makers are usually concerned with the quality of the services delivered to the public and they therefore cannot remain unconcerned about the number of employees in the public sector because most of these services are delivered by a labour-intensive process. Policy makers are concerned about teacher / pupil ratios, doctor / patient or population ratios and police / population ratios to give just three examples. It seems unlikely they will be content with controls on the pay bill alone. This means they are also likely to seek to control pay growth.

Public sector unions on the other hand may adopt an extreme form of insider behaviour and exhibit no concern for those who might loose their jobs.[8] Public sector unions may be less concerned about public sector employment than public sector wages and indeed a study from Sweden, Holmund (1997) found that cash limits were associated with higher unemployment. Under a system of cash limits, higher pay was bought at the price of lower unemployment. Thus, instead of imposing cash limits, policy makers, aware of these consequences, may seek mechanisms to directly control pay growth. Where this happens it usually results in a reduction in the dispersion of rates of pay growth.[9]

Conclusion

What conclusions can be drawn from the above and what are the implications for the countries studied here? The theory presented above suggests that a decentralised system presents a trade-off between containing pay growth on one hand and improving microeconomic efficiency on the other. The relative weight that countries attach to these arguments will be a critical determinant of which system a country adopts.

We noted above that the arguments in favour of decentralisation are likely to be weaker in the public sector than in the private sector. While intensified competition has driven private sector firms toward decentralised pay bargaining, these same pressures are absent in the public sector. We also noted that trade

---

[8] Dell'Aringa and Lanfranchi (1999) investigate the effects of different levels of bargaining on pay outcomes in the public sector. Although they concentrate on pay dispersion, their results show that, while decentralisation has a moderating effect on pay bill growth, decentralised public sectors do not necessarily moderate pay growth per employee, revealing that decentralisation affects the number employed as well as pay determination.

[9] For an analysis and history of government attempts to intervene in pay bargaining and the impact of such intervention of pay dispersion see Fallick and Elliott (1981).

union density is much greater in the public sector than in the private sector and that public sector unions may be able to resist moves to decentralised bargaining. Thus we might expect to observe rather less decentralisation in the public sector than in the private sectors, and indeed in Australia and the UK, decentralisation in the public sector has been largely confined to central government. In the subsequent country chapters, we shall see which of the above arguments for and against decentralisation appear to have been most important in each country.

The outcomes of decentralisation in central government are likely to be different from the outcomes we would observe in a decentralised system in the private sector for at least two reasons. First, during the period studied here, governments have sought to control the rate of pay growth. This has resulted in much less dispersion in the rates of pay growth than might otherwise have occurred under a decentralised system. In Sweden, central negotiations determined the rate of average pay growth while the distribution of the resulting amount was left to local negotiations. Though in theory there could still have been substantial variation around the centrally negotiated average rate of increase, in practice this tended not to happen. In the UK decentralised pay setting was monitored by the Treasury. Agencies and Departments had to have their bargaining strategy, their opening pay offer, approved by the Treasury, moreover, for a short period in the early nineties there was a limit on the permitted size of pay increase. Only in Australia was a more 'hands-off' approach adopted.

Second, unions have played a more prominent role in decentralised pay setting in the public sector than in the private sector. This will have had an important impact on pay outcomes for where unions play a role in pay setting considerations of equity and fairness are likely to play a prominent role. As a result, pay settlements will be less dispersed and pay structures flatter than would otherwise be the case.

For both the above reasons we are likely to find rather less dispersion in pay as a result of the move to decentralisation than occurred in the private sector. In the following pages we set out to discover just what happened to pay structures and to pay outcomes in the first few years after the introduction of these decentralised systems. We set out to identify and explain just how the pay structure in central government in these three countries changed after reforms were introduced in the early 1990s.

References

Arrow, D. J. (1974) *The Limits of Organization*, New York, Norton.

Bender, K. A. (1998) 'The Central Government-Private Sector Wage Differential,' *Journal of Economic Surveys*, 12(2): 177-220.

Brown, W., Marginson, P. and Walsh, J. (1991) 'Management: Pay Determination and Collective Bargaining' in P. Edwards (ed.), *Industrial Relations: Theory and Practice in Britain*, Oxford, Blackwell Publishers Ltd: 123-50.

Brown, W. and Walsh, J. (1991) 'Pay Determination in Britain in the 1980s: The Anatomy of Decentralization', *Oxford Review of Economic Policy*, 7(1): 44-59.

Calmfors, L. (1993) 'Centralization of Wage Bargaining and Macroeconomic Performance: A Survey', *OECD Economics Studies*, 21: 161-91.

Calmfors, L. and Driffil, J. (1988) 'Bargaining Structure, Corporatism and Macroeconomic Performance', *Economic Policy*, 6: 13-61.

Carruth, A. and Disney, R. (1988) 'Where Have Two Million Trade Union Members Gone?', *Economica*, 55: 1-19.

Dell'Aringa, C. and Lanfranchi, N. (1999) 'Pay Determination in the Public Service: An International Comparison' in R.F. Elliott, C. Lucifora, and D. Meurs (eds.), *Public Sector Pay Determination in the European Union*, London, Macmillan: 29-69.

Department of Education and Employment (1996) *Labour Market Trends*, London, HMSO.

Dowrick, S. (1993) 'Enterprise Bargaining, Union Structure and Wages', *Economic Record*, 69(207): 393-415.

Eichengreen, B. and Iversen, T. (1999) 'Institutions and Economic Performance: Evidence from the Labour Market', *Oxford Review of Economic Policy*, 15(4): 121-38.

Fallick, J. L. and Elliott, R. F. (1981) *Incomes, Policies, Inflation and Relative Pay*, London, George Allen and Unwin.

Flanagan, R. J. (1990) 'Centralised and Decentralised Pay Determination in Nordic Countries' in L. Calmfors (ed), *Wage Formation and Macroeconomic Policy in the Nordic Countries*, Oxford, Oxford University Press.

Flanagan, R. J. (1999) 'Macroeconomic Performance and Collective Bargaining: An International Perspective', *Journal of Economic Literature*, 37(3): 1150-95.

Freeman, R. B. (1980) 'Unionism and the Dispersion of Wages,' *Industrial and Labor Relations Review*, 34: 3-23.

Gottschalk, P. and Smeeding, T. M. (1997) 'Cross-national Comparisons of Earnings and Income Inequality', *Journal of Economic Literature*, 35(2): 633-87.

Gregory, R. G. and Borland, J. (1999) 'Recent Developments in Public Sector Labour Markets,' in O. Ashenfelter and D. Card (eds.), *Handbook of Labor Economics*, Volume 3C, Amsterdam, North-Holland: 3573-3630.

Holmlund, B. (1997) 'Macroeconomic Implications of Cash Limits in the Public Sector', *Economica*, 64(253): 49-62.

Holmlund, B. and Skedinger, P. (1990) 'Wage Bargaining and Wage Drift: Evidence from the Swedish Wood Industry' in Calmfors (ed.) op cit.

Jackson, M. P., Leopold, J. W., and Tuck, K. (1993) *Decentralization of Collective Bargaining: An Analysis of Recent Experience in the UK*. London, Macmillan

Jarley, P. and Kuruvilla, S. (1994) 'American Trade Unions and Public Approval: Can Unions Please All of the People All of the Time?', *Journal of Labor Research*, 15(2): 97-115.

Kahn, B. E. (1998) 'Dynamic Relationships with Customers: High-Variety Strategies', *Academy of Marketing Science*, 26(1): 45-53.

Katz, H. (1993) 'The Decentralization of Collective Bargaining: A Literature Review and Comparative Analysis', *Industrial and Labor Relations Review*, 47(1): 192-220.

Katz, L. F. and Krueger, A. B. (1993) 'Public Sector Pay Flexibility: Labor Market and Budgetary Considerations' *Pay Flexibility in the Public Sector*, Paris: OECD: 43-77.

Marsh, D., Edwards, P. K. and Bain, G. S. (1990) 'Public Opinion, Trade Unions and Mrs Thatcher; Trade Union Popularity, 1954-1988: A Reply to Marsh', *British Journal of Industrial Relations*, 28(1): 57-69.

Metcalf, D., Hansen, K. and Charlwood, A. (2000) 'Unions and the Sword of Justice: Unions and Pay Systems, Pay Inequality, Pay Discrimination and Low Pay', *Centre for Economic Performance*, Discussion Paper 452.

Millward, N., Stevens, M., Smart, D. and Hawes, W. R. (1992) *Workplace Industrial Relations in Transition: The ED/ESRC/PSI and ACAS Surveys*, Aldershot, England, Dartmouth.

Moene, K. O., Wallerstein, M. and Hoel, M. (1993) 'Bargaining Structure and Economic Performance' in R. J. Flanagan, K. O. Moene and M. Wallerstein (eds.) *Trade Union Behaviour, Pay Bargaining and Economic Performance*, Oxford, Clarendon Press: 63-131.

Organization for Economic Co-operation and Development (1994) *Employment Outlook*, July, Paris, OECD.

Organization for Economic Co-operation and Development (1996) *Employment Outlook*, July, Paris, OECD.

Organization for Economic Co-operation and Development (1997) *Employment Outlook*, July, Paris, OECD.

Piore, M. and Sabel, C. (1984) *The Second Industrial Divide*, New York, Basic Books.

Robinson, P. (1995) 'The Decline of the Swedish Model and the Limits to Active Labour Market Policy', *London School of Economics, Centre for Economic Performance*, Discussion Paper 259.

Rodseth, A. and Holden, S. (1990) 'Wage Formation in Norway' in Calmfors (ed) op cit.

Soskice, D. (1990) 'Wage Determination: The Changing Role of Institutions in Advanced Industrialized Countries', *Oxford Review of Economic Policy*, 6(4): 36-61.

Suen, W. (1991) 'The Value of Product Diversity', *Oxford Economic Papers*, 43(2): 217-23.

Walsh, G. (1988) 'Trade Unions And The Media', *International Labour Review*, 127(2): 205-21.

Walsh, J. (1993) 'Internalisation v. Decentralization: An Analysis of Recent Development in Pay Bargaining', *British Journal of Industrial Relations*, 31: 409-32.

Chapter 2

Data and Specification

Introduction

The period analysed here witnessed substantial changes in the organisational structure of the civil service in Australia, Sweden and the UK. These changes have in turn been accompanied by substantial changes in the composition of the civil service in each country, and thus any analysis of the resulting wage levels and wage structures requires access to detailed information on individual earnings and characteristics. Simply analysing movements in average pay levels and in the size of pay increases will obscure any changes in pay due to changes in the composition of the work force which have occurred.

An appropriate methodology for analysing individual level data is some form of multivariate analysis. Ordinary least squares (OLS) enables us to identify the returns (the coefficients) to different characteristics (the independent variables) and to distinguish how they change over time. Characteristics which we might employ to explain the variance of earnings (expressed in A\$, SKr and £), such as an employee's age, their length of service with a single department, and in the civil service as a whole, can be measured as continuous variables, in terms of years. Other characteristics can be identified by the use of dichotomous variables as for example, assigning dummy variables indicating where an individual works in a particular grade. Once the results from such regressions have been obtained, we can use procedures (discussed below) to decompose real pay changes over time in each of the three countries to distinguish that part of pay change which is accounted for by changes in the returns to employee characteristics (changes in the rewards to productive characteristics) and that part which is accounted for by changes in the characteristics themselves (changes in the composition).

In the next section of this chapter we detail the data sets that are used to analyse pay changes and pay structure in the civil services in each of the three countries. We list the sources of the data and their coverage and the strengths and weaknesses of each data set. The third section examines the variables used in the regression analysis and discusses comparisons of these variables across the countries while the fourth part elaborates the methodology used in the analysis. The next section summarises the particular specifications of the regression equations and details the different types of decomposition analysis used to distinguish how much of the change in average pay is attributable to changes to pay structure. A final part looks at the properties of the data. It looks at the mean values and at some other features of the data and thus provides a description of the main features of the civil service in each of the three countries in the years for which we undertake this analysis.

Data Sources

Detailed information on the earnings and characteristics of employees in the Civil Services of Australia, Sweden and the UK was obtained for two years, 1990 (1993 for Sweden) and 1996. The following three subsections detail the sources of the data from each of these countries, discuss the types of variables available in each dataset and outline the strengths and deficiencies of each data set.

Australia

The data on employees in the Australian Public Service (APS) comes from two data sets accessed on the authors' behalf and analysed as we requested by the Public Service and Merit Protection Commission (PSMPC) in Australia. The primary data file is called the Staffing Monitor System which contains information on pay (basic annual pay converted into monthly earnings), age, gender, agency or department affiliation, tenure in the APS, job classification and region of employment.[1] We have no information on individuals' hours of work since employers' payroll records only record these where this influences employees pay, i.e. when they are paid overtime, and very few APS employees are paid overtime. Merged to this data is educational qualification information from the Continuous Record of Personnel (CRP). Of the three countries studied, only in Australia do we have data on the educational qualifications of civil servants. The data is for the month of June in both 1990 and 1996.

The samples that we ultimately obtain are arrived at after several cuts in the data. Because we have no data on hours of work, we focus on only full-time permanent workers, thus we exclude part-timers, and where there was no information on any one of the variables for an individual we also discarded these observations. In the end we were left with 71,059 employees out of 136,392 in 1990 and 59,534 employees out of 128,548 in 1996.[2]

There are two weaknesses with the data. First, the information on educational qualifications is gathered only when the worker enters the APS. Updates are given voluntarily, or when required by the job and therefore the educational variable may understate the true educational qualifications of the

---

[1] Data on pay which is taken from employer payroll records, as distinct from being reported by the employee is likely to offer the most accurate recording of pay. It is thus a substantial advantage of this study that the data for all three countries is drawn from employers payroll records.

[2] The initial 1990 and 1996 samples are from the CRP data set which does not cover the entire APS. It does not include temporary workers and those in a small number of agencies not included under the Public Service Act.

worker. The magnitude of any bias that results will however be diminished by the fact that we aggregate the education qualifications into four main bands. Thus where there are only marginal improvements in qualifications which do not result in movements between the qualifications bands, individuals will continue to be assigned to the correct group. The second deficiency is that unlike the other two countries variables such as tenure with government department and agency are not available.

Sweden

The data on central government workers in Sweden comes from the Swedish Agency of Government Employers, the organisation which handles the employer's side of the wage negotiation process. The Swedish data provides information on basic monthly earnings and the gender and age of the employees. It also details the region and agency or department in which they work and their tenure in both central government and the agency. In one of the specifications we employ below, the 'country specific specification', monthly earnings have been adjusted to a full time equivalent basis using information on the percentage of full-time hours that employees work. However, in a second specification in which we employ a common template for all three countries, for purposes of comparison between the three countries, we analyse only full-time employees.

The analysis for Sweden is conducted over a somewhat shorter period than for the other two countries, since it extends from September 1993 to September 1996. The reason for this is that the occupational classification system currently in use, which is called the TNS system and which enables us to use a common scheme to classify occupations in all agencies, started in 1993. The analysis is therefore restricted to these years.

The TNS system assigns jobs into five major groups distinguished by level of responsibility. These are: expert or department manager; qualified administrator; administrator; qualified assistant, and assistant. In addition the TNS system allows us to distinguish a small group of the very highest ranking civil servants, managers of agencies and their equivalent, called senior civil servants hereafter. In the subsequent analysis, where we are dealing with the civil service as a whole, we distinguish these six occupational groupings.

As with the two other countries we delete observations where there have been coding errors or there is incomplete data. We also delete data for some organisations because Swedish central government includes many activities that might not be considered 'core' civil service activities and which are certainly not included in the range of civil service activities found in the other two countries. In Sweden the central government is, or has included, many public utilities and the railways, police, universities and the Church of Sweden. All these organisations are excluded in order to arrive at a civil service performing similar functions to those in the other two countries.

A final consideration affecting the sample size results from the use of TNS occupation classifications. The TNS system was set up to allow comparisons of jobs between the public and private sectors and it is only by using the TNS that jobs in central government can be grouped by level of responsibility. However, less than 70 per cent of central government employees had been classified by this system by 1996. For this reason the initial analysis was conducted using both a 'Full Sample' and the 'TNS Sample' where the latter included only those having jobs classified by the TNS system. The resulting samples were 136,423 and 109,302 for the 'Full Sample' in 1993 and 1996, respectively, and 76,864 and 65,173, respectively, for the TNS Samples in 1993 and 1996.

United Kingdom

The UK Civil Service data has been extracted from the Mandate database and was supplied by the Personnel Management and Conditions of Service Division of the Cabinet Office. This data set contains information on each employee's basic full-time equivalent annual earnings (converted to monthly for comparison with the other countries), the gender, age and race of the employee and the region, agency or department in which they work. Their tenure in the civil service and in the agency or department and their civil service grade are also recorded as is their marital status. The data is analysed for the years 1990 and 1996.

The criteria used to obtain the sample were similar to those used in the two previous cases. Observations with coding errors or incomplete data were deleted, and in the regressions using the common template we excluded part-time workers. Some of the smaller agencies (because of small sample sizes) and the Scottish and Welsh Offices were also excluded. The latter were excluded because they cover almost the complete range of activities covered by the English departments. They are therefore not as homogenous as the English departments and this is likely to result in greater wage variation in each of these Offices. In addition, there was no basic pay data recorded for the Office of Public Service, Foreign Office and Transport Departments in 1990 and the Foreign Office and Inland Revenue in 1996 which necessitated their exclusion from the data set. The resulting sample sizes after we have made these cuts are 302,477 out of 523,064 for 1990 and 338,207 out of 504,598 for 1996.

Differences in Levels of Aggregation of Departments and Agencies

The levels of disaggregation available in the three country data sets differ. More detail is available for Australia than for the other two countries. In the case of both Sweden and the UK, employees in the separate agencies that report to each central government department are recorded under that government department. Thus for example, in the UK, the employees recorded under the Department of Social Security include staff in the Benefits Agency and the Contribution Agency as well as those in the central government department itself. The agencies and departments listed for Sweden and the UK are thus more heterogeneous than in Australia. One consequence is that we should expect decentralisation to result in more intra-agency wage variation in Sweden and the UK than we will observe in Australia where the impact of decentralisation is likely to be captured in greater inter-agency wage dispersion.

Country Specific and Common Specification

The three datasets detailed above have several variables in common but they differ in some other important respects. Table 2.1 reports the characteristics of civil servants that are available in each of the three data sets. In the analysis in this book we use this data in two ways.

First, in the three country chapters which follow, Chapters 3, 4 and 5, we use the full set of variables available for each country. We call this the 'country specific specification' since it includes some variables which are only available for a particular country. Thus the educational attainment of civil servants is only available for Australia while ethnicity and marital status are only available for the UK. The length of time the individual has been employed in the civil service is available for only Sweden and the UK.

Second, we also use a 'Common Specification'. This common specification uses only those variables which are available for all three countries, and this ensures that when we contrast and compare developments in the three countries we are comparing like-with-like. This comparative analysis is the focus of Chapter 6.

This section details the data used in the regressions and compares the information across countries.

The Variables

Dependent Variable

The dependent variable in the regressions is (the natural log of) monthly basic pay. Basic pay was chosen in preference to actual pay for the latter may include additions for reimbursements for travel (in the case of Sweden) or sickness or maternity pay and may be distorted by one-off bonuses which may result in large and erratic movements in pay which are not typical. Pay was expressed in monthly terms because of the ease of converting the UK annual pay data and the Australian fortnightly data on to the same basis as the Swedish data.

Table 2.1 Independent Variables: Personal Characteristics and Educational Qualifications

Variable	Australia	Availability Sweden	UK	Definition
Personal Characteristics				
MALE*	yes	yes	yes	Employee is male
AGE*	yes	yes	yes	Employee's age
AGE2*	yes	yes	yes	Age squared
TENGOV*	yes	yes	yes	Years of tenure in government service
TENGOV2*	yes	yes	yes	Government tenure squared
TENAG	no	yes	yes	Years of tenure in agency or department
TENAG2	no	yes	yes	Agency or Department tenure squared
FULL	no	yes	yes	Employee is full-time
WHITE	no	no	yes*	Employee is white
MARRIED	no	no	yes*	Employee is married
REGION*	yes (8)[a]	yes (4)[b]	yes (11)[c]	Region of employment
Educational Qualifications				
ED0	yes	no	no	Low or no qualification
ED1	yes	no	no	Secondary school qualification only
ED2	yes	no	no	Post secondary school
ED3	yes	no	no	University

Notes: a.   * indicates part of the 'Common Specification'.

b.   The Australian regions are: Australian Capital Territories (ACT), New South Wales (NSW), Victoria (VIC), Queensland (QUEEN), South Australia (SA), Western Australia (WA), Tasmania (TAS) and the New Territories (NT).

c.   The Swedish regions are: Stockholm (STOCK), North (NORTH), Central (CENTRAL) and South (SOUTH).

d.   The British 'regions' are: Scotland (SCOT), North (NORTH), York and Humberside (YORKHUM), rest of the North West (NW), East Midlands (EMID), West Midlands (WMID), Wales (WALES), East Anglia (EANGLIA), South East (SE), South West (SW) and Northern Ireland (NI).

Part-timers are treated in a number of ways. In the common specification, the focus is on full-timers only in all three countries. However, in the country specific specification for Sweden we can calculate full-time equivalent pay because we know the percentage of full-time hours that part-time employees are contracted to work. Again in the UK country specific specification, we calculate the full-time pay equivalent. Therefore, part-time workers are included in the country specific regression for the UK and Sweden. However because we have no information on hours for Australian workers and therefore cannot construct a full-time pay measure, the Australian 'country specific' regressions focus on full-timers throughout. Other than the proportion of full-time hours contracted to be worked by part-timers in Sweden and the UK, we have no data on hours of work. However, we do know that civil servants rarely work paid overtime, and therefore that paid-for hours of work equal basic hours of work in the overwhelming majority of cases.

Independent Variables

There are four sets of variables which constitute the independent variables used in the analysis. These four sets are Personal Characteristics, Educational Qualifications, Job Classification and Agency or Department Affiliation.

Personal Characteristics These variables are summarised in Table 2.1. The gender identifier (MALE) is included to capture differences in pay between genders. A variety of reasons have been proffered in the economics literature to explain why there may be differences between the pay of males and females (see Altonji and Blank, 1999). Among these are differences in access to jobs, differences in the rates at which pay grows due to differences in labour force experience (the acquisition of general human capital), differences in tenure (the acquisition of specific human capital), differences in opportunities for promotions and finally discrimination. Although the limited data at our disposal means we are unable to test directly several of these explanations because gender variables are shown to play a significant role in explaining the variation in individual pay in most studies, we include an identifier for gender. An AGE variable is included to capture the growth in pay during an individuals working life. One of the reasons for this growth is that age can serve as a proxy for general labour market experience. This is particularly true of men but less true for women, many of whom will have taken a career break at some time during their working lives. Positively sloped age-pay (usually called age-earnings) profiles are a fairly robust empirical result in labour economics. In such specifications, a squared term is included to capture non-linearity's in these profiles and we follow this practice.

The next four variables shown in Table 2.1 are included to indicate the returns to specific human capital. They measure the length of employment in the civil service (TENGOV) and in the agency or department in which the individual is currently employed (TENAG). Again, the squared terms are included to capture non-linearities in these returns. Included in the estimates for the UK are variables indicating race and marital status since these have been shown to explain part of the difference between individual pay in other research (see Altonji and Blank, 1999). Finally, for each country a set of variables are included to indicate the region in which the individual works in order to capture any regional impact on pay beyond that captured in the variables we have already included.

Educational Qualifications   Only the Australian data included information on educational qualifications. The raw data identifies up to 15 different qualifications, but these were aggregated into four broad levels of qualifications to minimise the biases due to those unmeasured increases in educational attainment mentioned earlier.   The four resulting levels of education are: low or no qualifications; secondary school qualifications; post-secondary school qualification (diplomas, tertiary certificates, etc); and university qualifications. Educational qualifications measure returns to general human capital.

Job Classification   In each country the grades (occupations) were classified into a hierarchy which is the same in each country and therefore comparable between the three countries.   This was achieved by aggregating the different grades into a relatively small number of categories. The five categories are shown in Table 2.2 and are: highest ranking civil servants and department or agencies managers; senior officers, managers and senior executives; higher administrative grades and junior executives; the mainstream administrative grade and finally; administrative assistants. The definitions of the variables are given in the Notes to Table 2.2.

Department Affiliation   Individuals were identified by the government department in which they worked, and a list of these departments is shown in Table 2.3. This Table also shows the degree of correspondence between the departments in the three countries which is important for the comparative analysis conducted in Chapter 6.   Table 2.3 also shows the share of civil service employment accounted for by each of these large departments.   This is calculated as the average of the starting and end years in each data set, and because the table includes only the largest departments, the shares do not sum to 100. The difference between the total of the shares in Table 2.3 and 100 is of course accounted for by the smaller departments not shown.

In the case of Australia, we were also able to obtain details for each of the separate agencies and the smaller departments that comprise the Australian Public Service and therefore these are used in the country analysis in Chapter 3. However, in the case of Sweden and the UK, information at the detailed agency level was not always available and therefore employees are classified according to the 'host' department.

Table 2.2 Independent Variables: Occupation Classification

	Australia[a]	Sweden[b]	UK[c]	Definition
1	SES	HIGHCS, DEPTMAN	SENIORCS	The highest ranking civil servants, and Department and Agency managers
2	SO	QUALAD	HIGHCS	Senior Officers, Managers, Senior Executives
3	SO	ADMIN	EO	Higher Administrative Grades, Junior Executives
4	ASO	QUALASST	ADMIN	Mainstream Administrative Grades
5	GSO	ASST	ADMINAS	Administrative Assistants
6	OTHER	-	-	Not elsewhere classified

Notes: a. The variables stand for: SES - Senior service; SO - senior officer grade; ASO - administrative service officer; GSO - general service officer.

b. The variables stand for: HIGHCS - highest ranking civil servants (agency managers and equivalent); DEPTMAN - departmental managers and equivalent; QUALAD - qualified administrators; ADMIN - administrators; QUALASST - qualified assistants; ASST - assistants. Derived from TNS system.

c. The variables stand for: SENIORCS - Senior civil servants (grades 1-5); HIGHCS - high ranking civil servants (grades 6 and 7) and highest ranking executives; EO - executive officers; ADMIN - administration grades; ADMINAS - administration assistants.

Methodology

In this section we detail the methodology and variable specifications used in the analysis. In addition we describe the decomposition methods used to distinguish between changes in the characteristics of the civil service workforce and changes in the wage structure. The analysis is contained in the 'country' chapters, and in each of these chapters, the analysis has the following structure.

Examination of Raw Earnings Data

In each of the country specific chapters, we begin by investigating the raw earnings data to identify trends in the data during the early 1990s. Several different statistics are employed in the analysis. First, we examine the growth rate in real median earnings over time. We use the median rather than the mean because there were extremely low earnings levels recorded for some job classifications, particularly in the UK data in 1990.

Decentralised Pay Setting

**Table 2.3 Largest Departments and Agencies and their Correspondence
between the Three Countries**

Australia		Sweden		UK	
Attorney General	(2.2)	Justice	(13.2)	Courts	(3.6)
				Home Office	(13.3)
Defence	(16.0)	Defence	(27.1)	Defence	(18.2)
(Employment, Education)	(10.2)	Labour	(11.6)	(Education and Employment)*	(16.2)
Social Security	(15.3)	Social Affairs	(3.8)	Social Security	(29.6)
(Foreign Affairs and Trade)	(2.3)	Foreign Affairs	(3.0)		
Australian Taxation Office	(19.0)	(Finance)	(18.8)	H.M. Treasury	(0.5)
Customs	(5.4)	-	-	Customs and Excise	(7.4)
-	-	Environment	(2.7)	Environment	(1.5)
-	-	Culture	(4.3)	-	
(Employment, Education)	-	Education	(2.6)	(Education and Employment)*	
-	-	Transport	(1.3)	{Transport}	(3.4)
-	-	Agriculture	(3.3)	Agriculture, Fisheries and Food	(3.0)
(Foreign Affairs and Trade)	(see above)	Trade	(2.6)	Trade and Industry	(3.1)
				Health	(2.1)
Administrative Services	(4.9)	Public Affairs	(6.5)	{Cabinet Office}	(0.4)
Veteran Affairs	(4.0)	-	-	-	-

Notes: a. * indicates that in 1990 these had been different departments but by 1996 they had merged and for comparability they were therefore also amalgamated in our data set for 1990.

  b. Agencies in parentheses have responsibilities for a number of activities, which are the concern of a single department in the other countries.

  c. Numbers in parenthesis report the average share of total civil service employment accounted for across the two years 1990 and 1996 in Australia and the UK and across the two years 1993 and 1996 in Sweden. (See Tables 2.4, 2.5 and 2.6 following).

  d. Those UK departments shown in curly brackets are not featured in the subsequent analysis because data is not available for them in both years.

  e. The Australian data also includes several other small agencies which have no clear counterpart to agencies in the other two countries.

Analysing real average pay growth with these data led to very large increases for some job classifications and departments. It is unclear whether these extreme values were actual pay levels or coding errors, so rather than drop them from the analysis, we minimise their effect on the growth rate of pay by analysing changes in median pay.

We examine pay growth for the sample as a whole and for each of the main civil service grades and major departments. We seek to identify any differences in pay growth between grades and departments and to distinguish any differences by gender in order to determine whether reform affected men and women differently.

The pay reforms are likely to have changed both pay growth and pay dispersion because the reforms were designed to make pay structures more responsive to changes in pay in the private sectors of each of these countries. Earlier we saw that private sector pay dispersion increased in some of these countries, and it is therefore likely that public sector pay reform will have lead to increased pay dispersion and for this reason we also examine changes in the dispersion of real pay. We employ three measures. The first is the standard deviation, where changes in the standard deviation capture the change in the overall distribution of pay over time. The other two measures isolate the effects of reform on the lower and upper ends of the pay distribution. Changes in the ratio of the first decile to the median record changes that occurred at the lower end of the distribution. Changes in the ratio of the ninth decile to the median track changes that occurred at the upper end of the pay distribution. Different types of pay reform are likely to affect different parts of the pay distribution,[3] and therefore examining the changes at different points in the pay distribution can provide insights into the relative effects of pay reform.

OLS Specification

While a useful starting point, the examination of the raw data will not be able to identify all the consequences of the changes that have occurred in the systems of public sector pay determination for these three countries. For example the contracting out and privatisation of largely manual jobs that took place in the UK led to a more homogeneous, much more predominantly white collar, civil service. The effect of these changes in composition will have muted the influence of decentralisation and individualisation if for example, contracting led to a decrease in pay dispersion while the other reforms led to increases in pay dispersion. The raw data will confound the effects of contracting out, decentralisation and individualisation and although knowing the overall effect of pay reform is

---

[3] For example, contracting out and privatisation might have a relatively stronger effect on the pay of the least senior occupations in central government while the individualisation of pay may have a more pronounced effect on the pay of employees in the most senior occupations.

important, it is also important to understand how much of the overall changes result from each of these three types of reform.

To capture the relative effects of the three types of pay reform, we need to be able to control for changes in composition and to look at the wage structure in isolation of changes in composition. Therefore, we employ standard Ordinary Least Squares (OLS) multivariate regression techniques. The coefficients on the variables in the OLS regressions identify the magnitude of the rewards (returns) to each of the measured characteristics of the workforce. Thus, the general estimating form is:

$$\ln W_i^t = X_i^t \beta^t + R_i^t \alpha^t + D_i^t \gamma^t + G_i^t \varphi_i^t + \varepsilon_i^t,$$ (1)

where $\ln W$ is average monthly pay for individual i, X_i is a vector of personal and human capital variables (such as those detailed in section 3 above), R_i is a vector of regional indicators, D_i is a vector of departmental / agency indicators, G_i is a vector of civil service grade indicators and ε_i is a normal *iid* disturbance term all indexed at time t. The estimated coefficients or the returns, the β's,α's,γ's and φ's describe the pay structure in the civil service in each country for each year.

One property of the OLS estimator is that it assumes that the sample upon which it is based is representative of the underlying population or put another way, that it differs only randomly from other samples that might be drawn from that population. However, if there is some element of choice in the construction of the sample (either by the researcher or by the people in the sample) the OLS estimates may be biased. This will occur if the factors that determine that choice vary systematically across samples. This is known as the sample selection problem.

In our case, the civil servants, whose pay we seek to explain, may have different preferences for public sector employment, specific abilities or skills which may make them more productive in the public sector than in other jobs. Without controlling for these productive, yet unmeasured, characteristics, the OLS estimates will be biased.

On the face of it, sample selection is therefore a potentially serious problem. However, it is unlikely that sample selection will be a large problem here. First, all the employees we analyse here can be assumed to have the same unmeasured characteristics which determined the choice of public sector jobs. Therefore, comparing coefficients across countries will net out any sample selection biases. Second, because we compare different years, we again net out the biases in the coefficients, as long as the unmeasured characteristics that determined the public sector service have remained the same over the periods analysed.

We use two variable specifications for each country except Sweden where we use four specifications. In the first of these specifications, called the *Common Specification* the same variables are used in all three countries for full-time workers only. This specification comprises a constant term and the variables MALE, AGE, AGE2, TENGOV, TENGOV2 and REGION (see the notes to Table 2.1), together with the grade classification indicator (see Table 2.2) and the departmental affiliation (see Table 2.3).[4]

A second specification was also employed for each country. This *Country Specific Specification* includes all the other variables that are available in each of the different country data sets. This specification therefore contains all the variables from the Common Specification plus the following variables: the education variables (for Australia). TENAG (for Sweden and the UK), TENAG2 (for Sweden and the UK), FULL (for Sweden and the UK), WHITE (for UK) and MARRIED (for UK). As in the Common Specification, the Swedish data is run on both the full sample with no occupational classification and the TNS sample. In addition, full time equivalent monthly pay is used in the Swedish and UK regressions. The *country specific specification* forms the basis of the analysis in Chapters 3 to 5.

Earlier studies have revealed that the pay structures for males and females in the public sector are very different, (see for example, Gregory, 1990, Bender 1998 and Bender and Elliott, 2002). Therefore after we have run the regressions for all employees we run separate regressions for females and males.

Decomposition Analysis

Once we have run these regressions, we can use the estimated coefficients to analyse the effects of changes in the pay structure on average pay. Decentralisation might be expected to change the pay structure. It might lead to greater dispersion in the pay of different grades as agencies address the double imbalance or it might lead to a greater dispersion in pay between departments if the pace or nature of reform differs between departments. Using a method proposed by Oaxaca we can distinguish the degree to which pay change is accounted for by changes in pay structure as distinct from changes in the characteristics, the composition, of the workforce in the different departments. Following Oaxaca (1973) first define average pay, $\overline{w}$, by:

$$\ln\overline{W}^t = Z^t \hat{\varphi}^t \tag{2}$$

and

$$\ln\overline{W}^{t-1} = Z^{t-1} \hat{\varphi}^{t-1} \tag{3}$$

---

[4] Recall that in Sweden grades can only be identified if the TNS classification system is used. When the system was used here, it resulted in the loss of some observations due to the existence of jobs which were not classified by TNS. In this chapter, we explore the differences between the sample of Swedish civil servants when we used the TNS classification system and when we do not. However, in Chapter 4 where we examine the Swedish data using the 'Country Specific Specification' and in Chapter 6 where we use the 'Common Specification', we restrict the sample to only those covered by the TNS classification. This is because we wish to examine the effect of reform on the grade pay structure.

where $\mathbf{Z}$ is a vector of variables taken at their respective means, $\hat{\phi}$ is a vector of estimated coefficients and t and $t\text{-}1$ index the current and previous time periods. Subtracting (3) from (2), one can decompose changes in average pay as:

$$Z^t\hat{\phi}^t - Z^{t-1}\hat{\phi}^{t-1} = Z^t(\hat{\phi}^t - \hat{\phi}^{t-1}) + (Z^t - Z^{t-1})\hat{\phi}^{t-1} \tag{4}$$

or

$$Z^t\hat{\phi}^t - Z^{t-1}\hat{\phi}^{t-1} = Z^{t-1}(\hat{\phi}^t - \hat{\phi}^{t-1}) + (Z^t - Z^{t-1})\hat{\phi}^t. \tag{5}$$

In both of these different weighting schemes the first term on the right hand side of the equal sign measures the contribution of the changing pay structure (returns) to the change in average pay while the second term measures the contribution of changes in average characteristics. Evidently the contribution of the changing pay structure can be weighted by either the current or previous distribution of characteristics, $\mathbf{Z^t}$ or $\mathbf{Z^{t-1}}$ respectively. The problem of selecting the weights is common to this methodology and is known as the index number of problem. Unfortunately, theory gives no clear guide as to which weighting scheme is the appropriate one. Where the data allows, we have used the method suggested by Reimers (1983) which averages the two weighting schemes together. This has the following formulation:

$$Z^t\hat{\phi}^t - Z^{t-1}\hat{\phi}^{t-1} = 0.5(Z^t + Z^{t-1})(\hat{\phi}^t - \hat{\phi}^{t-1}) + 0.5(Z^t - Z^{t-1})(\hat{\phi}^t + \hat{\phi}^{t-1}) \tag{6}$$

Again the first term to the right of the equals sign captures the effect of changes in pay structure while the second term captures the effect of changes in characteristics on the change in average pay.

Finally, we can decompose $\mathbf{Z^t}$ into the four groups of variables found in equation (1) (Personal Characteristics, Region, Occupation, and Department / Agency) to determine the relative importance of these different groups on the change in average wages.

Properties of the Data

It is instructive to look in some detail at the properties of data used in the subsequent analysis for this helps distinguish some of the more important general features of the structure of pay in the civil services of the three countries analysed here. We report the properties of the samples in both the start and end years, which are used in the analysis in the following chapters distinguishing first all employees and then men and women separately.

Australia

Table 2.4 contains the summary statistics of the variables for the Australian data. The first row contains the median values of real monthly earnings, which reveals that in the Australian Civil Service males were paid more than females in both years analysed and that their pay was more dispersed as revealed by the standard deviations reported in parenthesis. This 'unadjusted' gap, that is it takes no account of differences in the characteristics of men and women, decreased from 35.4 to 11.0 per cent between 1990 and 1996.[5] Over the six years the real average monthly pay of all employees increased by 17.5 per cent overall, but female average pay increased by 28.9 per cent while male pay increased by 5.7 per cent.

The rest of Table 2.4 contains averages for the other variables available for the Australian data. Males make up a majority of the sample: over 60.8 per cent in 1996, up from 59.5 per cent in 1990. Males have substantially higher levels of tenure in government service and are older than their female counterparts in 1990 and 1996. Again, the gap has narrowed somewhat over the six years, and the average length of time spent in government employment has increased quite sharply over the period as employment in the civil service contracted.

Average levels of education have increased over time: over 24 per cent possessed a university degree in 1996 compared to 20 per cent in 1990, and there are fewer with the lowest levels of education in 1996. There are significant differences in educational attainment between males and females. A higher proportion of men than women possess a university degree, 23.4 per cent of men in 1990 compared to 15.2 per cent of women. By 1996 the gap had narrowed to 26.7 per cent and 23.4 per cent, respectively.

Unsurprisingly, most of the central government workers were employed in either the Australian Capital Territory (ACT) (Canberra), New South Wales (NSW) or Victoria (Vic) although by 1996 there had been a consolidation to the ACT such that 31 per cent of all civil servants worked in Canberra. The largest agencies are the Department of Veterans Affairs (DVA), Social Security (SOCSEC), Customs, the Australian Taxation Office (ATO) (the largest), Defense, Employment, Education and Youth Affairs (DEETYA) and Administrative Services (ADMIN). Finally, over half of the employees are in the grade ASO, with around 80 of all females found in this occupational group. Males are more highly represented in the higher levels of the civil service, in the SES and SO groups.

---

[5] Percentage differences or changes are calculated by taking the inverse natural log of the difference in log monthly earnings.

Table 2.4 Summary Statistics of Australian Data: Country Specific Specification

	1990			1996		
	All Employees	Male	Female	All Employees	Male	Female
LMONTHLY	7.823	7.947	7.644	7.984	8.002	7.898
	(0.325)	(0.324)	(0.280)	(0.298)	(0.294)	(0.273)
Personal Characteristics						
MALE	0.595	1.000	0.000	0.608	1.000	0.000
AGE	35.670	37.499	32.988	39.657	40.981	37.606
	(9.445)	(9.108)	(9.289)	(8.989)	(8.706)	(9.036)
AGESQ	1361.580	1489.120	1174.520	1653.510	1755.290	1495.840
	(723.349)	(720.439)	(685.973)	(727.861)	(718.232)	(714.470)
TENGOV	9.300	11.234	6.464	12.998	14.657	10.429
	(7.500)	(8.269)	(4.994)	(8.156)	(8.902)	(5.995)
TENGOVSQ	142.741	194.575	66.719	235.468	294.068	144.698
ED0	0.283	0.187	0.424	0.248	0.170	0.368
ED1	0.408	0.444	0.355	0.401	0.437	0.345
ED2	0.109	0.136	0.070	0.109	0.126	0.083
ED3	0.200	0.234	0.152	0.242	0.267	0.204
Region						
Capital Terr.	0.269	0.284	0.248	0.310	0.320	0.294
New S. Wales	0.231	0.217	0.250	0.216	0.204	0.235
Victoria	0.209	0.216	0.199	0.188	0.197	0.175
Queensland	0.105	0.094	0.123	0.105	0.094	0.123
S. Australia	0.082	0.087	0.074	0.079	0.084	0.072
W. Australia	0.059	0.057	0.061	0.055	0.054	0.056
Tasmania	0.023	0.023	0.023	0.021	0.021	0.021
N. Territories	0.014	0.012	0.015	0.012	0.010	0.016
Agency / Departmental Indicators						
ATT GEN	0.027	0.022	0.034	0.017	0.015	0.020
AIPO	6.56E-3	6.86E-3	6.11E-3	6.89E-3	7.24E-3	6.34E-3
ACCC	1.72E-3	1.87E-3	1.49E-3	2.69E-3	3.01E-3	2.18E-3
PSMPRA	2.10E-3	1.35E-3	3.19E-3	2.18E-3	1.60E-3	3.08E-3
AIDAB	4.97E-3	5.56E-3	4.10E-3	5.12E-3	5.45E-3	4.62E-3
AGPS	3.97E-3	4.35E-3	3.40E-3	2.27E-3	2.54E-3	1.84E-3
ATSIC	7.12E-3	7.46E-3	6.63E-3	6.52E-3	5.89E-3	7.49E-3
AWM	1.28E-3	1.30E-3	1.25E-3	1.36E-3	1.47E-3	1.20E-3
NCA	2.25E-3	1.78E-3	2.95E-3	2.79E-3	2.21E-3	3.68E-3
AGSO	4.90E-3	6.96E-3	1.87E-3	4.20E-3	6.05E-3	1.33E-3
NLA	4.77E-3	2.86E-3	7.57E-3	4.87E-3	2.71E-3	8.22E-3
PMC	5.01E-3	4.00E-3	6.49E-3	4.67E-3	3.57E-3	6.38E-3
ANAO	7.12E-3	8.80E-3	4.65E-3	4.79E-3	5.64E-3	3.47E-3
DVA	0.056	0.050	0.065	0.025	0.024	0.026
WEATHER	0.013	0.018	4.79E-3	0.014	0.019	4.50E-3

Table 2.4 (Contd.)

	1990			1996		
	All Employees	Male	Female	All Employees	Male	Female
AEC	6.8E-3	7.10E-3	6.35E-3	7.36E-	7.71E-3	36.81E-3
SOCSEC	0.146	0.105	0.206	0.160	0.120	0.222
ARCHIVES	3.26E-3	3.24E-3	3.30E-3	2.94E-3	2.79E-3	3.17E-3
INDCOM	2.41E-3	2.44E-3	2.36E-3	2.47E-3	2.65E-3	2.18E-3
TREASURY	4.91E-3	5.47E-3	4.10E-3	6.55E-3	7.66E-3	4.84E-3
DPP	3.80E-3	3.36E-3	4.44E-3	3.21E-3	2.85E-3	3.77E-3
COMSUPER	4.93E-3	3.95E-3	6.35E-3	4.28E-3	3.68E-3	5.22E-3
ABS	0.033	0.035	0.030	0.035	0.037	0.033
CUSTOMS	0.052	0.062	0.036	0.055	0.066	0.037
ATO	0.183	0.174	0.197	0.196	0.191	0.203
DEFENCE	0.157	0.183	0.120	0.163	0.194	0.116
FINANCE	8.91E-3	0.010	7.91E-3	0.010	0.010	8.99E-3
HEALTH	1.66E-3	1.35E-3	2.12E-3	1.81E-3	1.71E-3	1.97E-3
ANCA	1.34E-3	1.61E-3	9.37E-3	2.33E-3	2.32E-3	2.35E-3
DIR	8.75E-3	9.30E-3	7.95E-3	5.63E-3	5.67E-3	5.57E-3
DEETYA	0.093	0.083	0.106	0.112	0.095	0.138
DPIE	0.028	0.038	0.014	0.022	0.029	0.012
DFAT	0.022	0.025	0.018	0.025	0.028	0.021
ADMIN	0.059	0.073	0.038	0.039	0.048	0.024
IMMIG	0.024	0.021	0.029	0.032	0.028	0.037
ABARE	2.70E-3	3.55E-3	1.46E-3	2.54E-3	2.82E-3	2.10E-3
ISC	1.70E-3	1.66E-3	1.77E-3	4.77E-3	4.42E-3	5.31E-3
COMCARE	3.55E-3	2.93E-3	4.44E-3	2.86E-3	2.82E-3	2.91E-3
Grades						
SES	0.016	0.024	3.64E-3	0.019	0.026	7.54E-3
SO	0.097	0.132	0.047	0.142	0.177	0.087
ASO	0.668	0.544	0.849	0.619	0.508	0.791
GSO	0.026	0.038	0.010	0.016	0.025	3.30E-3
OTHER	0.192	0.262	0.090	0.204	0.264	0.111
No. of cases	71059	42251	28808	59534	36178	23356

Notes:
a. The summary statistic for LNMONTHLY is the (natural log of) median monthly earnings, in 1990 Australian dollars. All other summary statistics not in parentheses are means.
b. Figures in parentheses are standard deviations.
c. The full titles of the agencies and departments are given in Appendix 3.2 to Chapter 3 on Australia.

Sweden

Tables 2.5 and 2.6 contain, respectively, the summary statistics of the variables for the full sample and sample which can be classified under TNS for Sweden. Table 2.5 reveals that median monthly pay for males in 1993 were about 13.3 per cent more than females and that by 1996 this unadjusted pay difference had fallen slightly to 13.0 per cent. Real median pay increased by 6.4 per cent for all employees, 6.5 per cent for females and 6.2 per cent for males from 1993 to 1996. In both years the pay of males was more dispersed than that of females as reflected in the larger standard deviations for the former. In contrast to Australia, males in the Swedish civil service are slightly younger than women yet despite this, in 1993, they had longer tenure in government service. It is also clear however, that within government, they are more likely to change jobs than are women because they have less tenure in the agency than do women. More males are employed full time than are women and the proportion of full-time workers rose between 1993 and 1996. A very high proportion of male employment is to be found in the Ministries of Defence, Justice and Finance, while female employment is concentrated in these same ministries and Labour.

Table 2.5 Summary Statistics of Swedish Data using the Full Sample: Country Specific Specification

	1990			1996		
	All Employees	Male	Female	All Employees	Male	Female
LMONTHLY	9.550	9.491	9.616	9.612	9.554	9.676
	(0.269)	(0.203)	(0.301)	(0.468)	(0.437)	(0.486)
Personal Characteristics						
MALE	0.543	0.000	1.000	0.518	0.000	1.000
AGE	43.192	43.526	42.911	43.787	44.363	43.251
	(11.272)	(10.934)	(11.542)	(10.817)	(10.558)	(11.026)
AGESQ	1992.640	2014.037	1974.604	2034.321	2079.559	1992.171
	(974.772)	(944.672)	(999.091)	(938.088)	(923.173)	(949.844)
TENGOV	14.775	14.459	15.042	15.145	15.162	15.128
	(10.879)	(10.591)	(11.109)	(11.276)	(11.158)	(11.386)
TENGOVSQ	336.646	321.211	349.656	356.512	354.381	358.497
	(395.298)	(385.189)	(403.166)	(435.808)	(431.517)	(439.764)
TENAG	7.946	9.9096	6.977	8.948	10.104	7.870
	(7.411)	(7.658)	(7.051)	(9.075)	(9.256)	(8.768)
TENAGSQ	118.061	141.395	98.392	162.422	187.757	138.817
	(165.568)	(175.605)	(155.787)	(277.376)	(289.752)	(263.142)
FULL	0.825	0.729	0.905	0.844	0.764	0.919
Region						
Stockholm	0.285	0.300	0.271	0.317	0.325	0.307
South Region	0.219	0.205	0.231	0.208	0.199	0.217
Central Region	0.309	0.321	0.299	0.308	0.315	0.303
North Region	0.187	0.174	0.199	0.167	0.161	0.173

Table 2.5 (Contd.)

	1990			1996		
	All Employees	Male	Female	All Employees	Male	Female
Departmental Indicators						
JUSTICE	0.122	0.142	0.104	0.143	0.160	0.160
FORAFF	0.020	0.024	0.016	0.039	0.050	0.050
DEFENSE	0.313	0.151	0.450	0.229	0.089	0.089
SOCIALAF	0.018	0.024	0.013	0.057	0.059	0.059
TRANSPORT	0.013	0.011	0.014	0.012	0.009	0.009
FINANCE	0.180	0.244	0.126	0.195	0.251	0.251
EDUC	0.021	0.032	0.012	0.030	0.042	0.042
AGRI	0.044	0.029	0.058	0.022	0.023	0.023
LABOUR	0.114	0.145	0.089	0.118	0.150	0.150
CULTURE	0.058	0.077	0.043	0.027	0.030	0.030
TRADE	0.015	0.018	0.012	0.037	0.033	0.033
PUBAFF	0.049	0.065	0.035	0.081	0.093	0.093
ENVIRON	0.033	0.038	0.028	0.010	0.011	0.011
No. of Cases	136423	63297	74026	109302	52719	52719

Notes: a.   The summary statistic for LNMONTHLY is the (natural log of) median monthly earnings, in 1993 Swedish Kroner. All other summary statistics not in parentheses are means.

b.   Figures in parentheses are standard deviations.

c.   The full titles of the agencies and departments are given in Appendix 4.1 to Chapter 4 on Sweden.

The sample of employees who are classified under the TNS system, Table 2.6, reveals very similar patterns to Table 2.5. There is again higher and more dispersed pay for males although the gap in median monthly pay between men and women is now bigger at 21.3 per cent in 1993 and 20.0 per cent in 1996. Real median pay increased by 5.8, 6.2 and 5.0 per cent for all employees, females and males. One of the features of the TNS sample is that a much smaller share of total employment is to be found in the Labour department (which had its own occupational classification system and did not therefore, for the most part, use TNS) and a larger share in Finance, which made extensive use of TNS. It is also clear from a comparison between Table 2.5 and 2.6 that the change in the shares of employment accounted for by these departments has a significantly different impact on the employment patterns of men and women which would appear to have much to do with the change in magnitude of the overall gender pay gap.

**Table 2.6 Summary Statistics of Swedish Data using the Sample with TNS
Classification: Country Specific Specification**

	1990			1996		
	All Employees	Male	Female	All Employees	Male	Female
LMONTHLY	9.569	9.487	9.680	9.625	9.547	9.729
	(0.252)	(0.191)	(0.271)	(0.291)	(0.252)	(0.303)
Personal Characteristics						
MALE	0.487	0.000	1.000	0.491	0.000	1.000
AGE	44.321	44.242	44.405	44.887	45.253	44.508
	(10.339)	(10.396)	(10.279)	(10.073)	(9.952)	(10.183)
AGESQ	2071.29	2065.393	2077.496	2116.336	2146.864	2084.663
	(905.625)	(908.001)	(903.088)	(888.002)	(880.775)	(894.35)
TENGOV	16.584	16.161	17.029	17.352	17.447	17.253
	(10.437)	(10.468)	(10.385)	(10.742)	(10.811)	(10.669)
TENGOVSQ	383.945	370.753	397.829	416.462	421.267	411.478
	(400.898)	(402.071)	(399.176)	(419.026)	(7426.885)	(416.026)
TENAG	9.710	10.564	8.812	9.959	11.240	8.630
	(7.533)	(7.596)	(7.36)	(9.199)	(9.411)	(8.779)
TENAGSQ	151.030	169.286	131.815	183.802	214.891	151.548
	(178.459)	(181.573)	(173.055)	(292.452)	(309.689)	(269.666)
FULL	0.831	0.723	0.945	0.863	0.775	0.954
Region						
Stockholm	0.304	0.322	0.286	0.337	0.355	0.318
South	0.213	0.200	0.227	0.212	0.189	0.237
Central	0.308	0.314	0.301	0.291	0.303	0.279
North	0.175	0.164	0.186	0.160	0.153	0.166
Departmental Indicators						
JUSTICE	0.051	0.085	0.015	0.056	0.093	0.018
FORAFF	0.028	0.032	0.024	0.053	0.063	0.042
DEFENSE	0.268	0.145	0.397	0.230	0.093	0.372
SOCIALAF	0.022	0.025	0.018	0.031	0.035	0.026
TRANSPORT	0.014	0.011	0.017	0.017	0.013	0.022
FINANCE	0.291	0.354	0.225	0.311	0.381	0.238
EDUC	0.029	0.040	0.017	0.039	0.055	0.023
AGRI	0.047	0.032	0.062	0.025	0.232	0.026
LABOUR	0.046	0.040	0.052	0.026	0.028	0.024
CULTURE	0.062	0.073	0.050	0.032	0.034	0.031
TRADE	0.020	0.023	0.018	0.052	0.042	0.063
PUBAFF	0.071	0.086	0.056	0.115	0.126	0.103
ENVIRON	0.051	0.054	0.049	0.013	0.014	0.012
Grades						
HIGHCS	0.005	0.002	0.009	0.007	0.003	0.011
DEPTMAN	0.029	0.010	0.050	0.029	0.013	0.046
QUALAD	0.115	0.058	0.174	0.123	0.073	0.175

Table 2.6 (Contd.)

	1990			1996		
	All Employees	Male	Female	All Employees	Male	Female
ADMIN	0.258	0.196	0.324	0.298	0.256	0.341
QUALASST	0.294	0.312	0.276	0.323	0.356	0.289
ASST	0.299	0.422	0.167	0.220	0.299	0.138
No. of Cases	76864	39415	37449	65173	33186	31987

Notes: a. The summary statistic for LNMONTHLY is the (natural log of) median monthly earnings, in 1993 Swedish Kroner. All other summary statistics not in parentheses are means.

b. Figures in parentheses are standard deviations.

c. The full titles of the agencies and departments are given in Appendix 4.1 to Chapter 4 on Sweden.

The TNS sample is the only one which allows us to distinguish the grade structure of the Swedish civil service. Again, we observe that men occupy a larger proportion of the highest grades; 5.9 per cent of males were employed in the two highest groups, highest ranking civil servants, (HIGHCS) and departmental managers (DEPTMAN), in 1993 compared to 1.2 per cent of women's employment in the same year. These two grades accounted for only 3.4 per cent of total employment in 1993. By 1996 the position of women had improved slightly: the share of women's employment in these two groups had risen from 1.2 to 1.6 per cent.

At the other end of the grade hierarchy there had been a corresponding improvement in the position of women, with only 29.9 per cent of women's total employment concentrated in the lowest group, assistants, in 1996 compared to 42.2 per cent in 1993. However, it is still the case that women's employment remains heavily concentrated in the lowest two occupational groups, assistants and qualified assistants, which together accounted for 73.4 and 65.5 per cent of women's employment in 1993 and 1996, respectively. In contrast these two groups accounted for 44.3 and 42.7 per cent, of men's employment in 1993 and 1996.

Table 2.7 Summary Statistics of the UK Data: Country Specific Specification

	1990			1996		
	All Employees	Male	Female	All Employees	Male	Female
LMONTHLY	6.574	6.54	6.877	6.733	6.677	7.005
	(0.47)	(0.43	(0.47)	(0.38)	(0.31)	(0.41)
Personal Characteristics						
MALE	0.46	0.00	1.00	0.46	0.00	1.00
WHITE	0.74	0.77	0.70	0.80	0.78	0.81
AGE	37.54	35.85	39.46	38.51	37.09	40.13
	(11.83)	(11.67	(11.72)	(10.77)	(10.40)	(10.96)
AGESQ	1549.73	1421.69	1694.74	1599.68	1483.90	1730.76
	(942.49)	(914.49	(952.67)	(870.22)	(822.81)	(903.22)
GOVTEN	10.68	8.71	12.91	11.02	9.75	12.45
	8.96	7.34	10.04	8.92	7.71	9.92
GOVTENSQ	194.54	129.82	267.84	201.09	154.69	253.63
	(286.30)	(202.58	(343.80)	(278.51)	(214.94)	(328.45)
FULL	0.928	0.87	0.99	0.88	0.79	0.98
Region						
South East	0.387	0.354	0.425	0.361	0.331	0.395
Scotland	0.068	0.076	0.059	0.070	0.074	0.065
North	0.081	0.092	0.070	0.077	0.089	0.062
York Humber	0.076	0.077	0.074	0.078	0.079	0.077
North West	0.122	0.132	0.110	0.129	0.145	0.111
E. Midland	0.049	0.047	0.050	0.044	0.045	0.043
W. Midland	0.066	0.072	0.060	0.067	0.072	0.062
Wales	0.041	0.046	0.036	0.041	0.045	0.037
E. Anglia	0.027	0.024	0.030	0.033	0.030	0.037
South West	0.078	0.076	0.081	0.094	0.084	0.106
N. Ireland	0.005	0.005	0.005	0.006	0.006	0.006
Departmental Indicators						
SOCSEC	0.282	0.356	0.198	0.310	0.396	0.213
MAFF	0.032	0.027	0.037	0.028	0.025	0.032
CABINET	0.005	0.005	0.004	0.004	0.004	0.004
TREASURY	0.008	0.007	0.010	0.003	0.002	0.004
CUSTOMS	0.088	0.064	0.115	0.059	0.049	0.070
DEFENSE	0.163	0.160	0.166	0.202	0.147	0.264
DFEE	0.174	0.212	0.131	0.150	0.198	0.096
DOE	0.012	0.010	0.015	0.027	0.022	0.032
HEALTH	0.030	0.027	0.032	0.013	0.013	0.012
HOMEOFF	0.132	0.058	0.216	0.135	0.071	0.208
COURTS	0.036	0.042	0.030	0.036	0.044	0.027
HERITAGE	2.0E-04	1.7E-04	2.3E-04	0.003	0.002	0.003
DTI	0.038	0.031	0.045	0.031	0.028	0.034

Table 2.7 (Contd.)

	1990			1996		
	All Employees	Male	Female	All Employees	Male	Female
Grades						
GRADE1	6.3E-05	0.0E+00	1.3E-04	6.2E-05	1.1E-05	1.2E-04
GRADE2	2.0E-04	2.5E-05	4.1E-04	2.0E-04	3.3E-05	3.9E-04
GRADE3	8.6E-04	1.4E-04	1.7E-03	8.3E-04	2.1E-04	1.5E-03
GRADE4	4.7E-04	8.7E-05	9.0E-04	4.5E-04	1.7E-04	7.6E-04
GRADE5	0.004	1.2E-03	0.007	0.004	1.4E-03	0.007
GRADE6	0.006	0.002	0.012	0.006	0.002	0.011
GRADE7	0.023	0.005	0.044	0.023	0.008	0.039
SENCS	0.044	0.010	0.082	0.039	0.014	0.067
HIGHCS	0.096	0.043	0.156	0.089	0.050	0.133
EO	0.215	0.199	0.233	0.228	0.212	0.246
ADMIN	0.422	0.481	0.355	0.437	0.503	0.362
ADMINAS	0.188	0.258	0.107	0.173	0.209	0.133
No of Cases	**302,477**	**160,636**	**141,841**	**338,207**	**179,585**	**158,622**

Notes: a.   The summary statistic for LNMONTHLY is the (natural log of) median monthly earnings, in 1990 British pounds. All other summary statistics not in parentheses are means.

        b.   Figures in parenthesis are standard deviation.

        c.   The full titles of the agencies and departments are given in Appendix 5.1 to Chapter 5

United Kingdom

Table 2.7 reveals that in the UK men had higher median pay than women. The raw 'unadjusted' gender pay gap was 40.1 in 1990 but fell to 38.8 per cent in 1996. Male civil servants are older than women and on average have been employed in the civil service longer than women, 12.9 years as compared to 8.7 in 1990 but this difference had narrowed by 1996 to 12.5 and 9.8 for men and women, respectively. However, unlike Sweden, the other country for which this data is available, men seem to change departments or agencies less frequently than do women. The vast majority of staff work full-time, and although as before the incidence of part-time working is higher among women than among men, in 1990, 87 per cent of women worked full-time. It is nonetheless striking that by 1996 the proportion of women working full-time had fallen to 79.2 per cent.

     The Ministry of Defence and the Departments of Employment and Education, which we saw were combined between 1990 and 1996, together with the Department of Social Security are the largest employers, with the latter alone accounting for 35.6 per cent of women's employment in 1990 rising to 39.6 per cent by 1996. Again we see, women's employment is heavily concentrated in the lowest occupational grades of administrative assistant, ADMINAS, and administrative officer, ADMIN, with these two grades accounting for 74 per cent of employment in 1990, down slightly to 71 per cent in 1996. The regional pattern of employment reveals what might have been anticipated, that employment is heavily concentrated in the South East, which includes London. However, 13 per cent of all women in 1990 rising to 14.5 per cent in 1996 were employed in the North West of England. It is noteworthy, that women's employment reveals slightly more regional dispersion than does men's.

The Three Countries Compared

The raw data in Tables 2.4, 2.5, 2.6 and 2.7 reveal a number of interesting contrasts between the three countries. First the raw 'unadjusted' pay gap between men and women is least in Sweden and substantially greater but very similar in the other two countries. This is in large part a reflection of the grade or occupational composition of civil service employment in the three countries. For while in all three countries very few women are employed in the very highest grades in Sweden a much larger proportion of women's employment is accounted for by the middle ranking grades. Sixty per cent of all civil servants were male in Australia in 1996 compared 52 per cent in Sweden and 47 per cent in the UK.

Sweden is also rather different from the other two countries with respect to the geographical distribution of civil service employment. While in all three countries the capital cities of Canberra, Stockholm and London account for a substantial share of total civil service employment, civil service employment is much more heavily concentrated in the region containing the capital in the UK and Australia than in Sweden.

It is also noteworthy that the average age of civil servants at around 44 in 1996 is considerably higher in Sweden than in either the UK or Australia at 39 and 40 years, respectively. Perhaps in consequence, employees in Sweden had by 1996 worked for an average of 15 years compared to an average of 13 years in Australia and 11 in the UK.

The above identifies some of the differences between the three countries. In the next three chapters we look in detail at the experience of each country separately. In Chapter 6 we then expand substantially the comparative analysis begun above.

References

Altonji, J. G. and Blank, R. M. (1999) 'Race and Gender in the Labor Market', in O. Ashenfelter and D. Card (eds.), *Handbook of Labor Economics*, Volume 3C Amsterdam, North-Holland: 3143-259.

Bender, K. A. (1998) 'The Central Government-Private Sector Wage Differential,' *Journal of Economic Surveys*, 12(2): 177-220.

Bender, K. A. and Elliott, R. F. (2002) 'The Role of Job Attributes in Understanding the Public-Private Sector Wage Differential in Britain', *Industrial Relations*, 41(3): 407-21.

Gregory, M. B. (1990) 'Public Sector Pay' in M. B. Gregory and A. W. J. Thomson (eds.) *A Portrait of Pay*, Oxford, Clarendon Press: 172-205.

Oaxaca, R. (1973) 'Male-Female Wage Differentials in Urban Labor Markets', *International Economic Review*, 14: 693-709.

Reimers, C. (1983) 'Labor Market Discrimination against Hispanic and Black Men', *Review of Economics and Statistics*, 65: 570-79.

Chapter 3

Australia

Introduction

In the mid 1990s, the civil service in Australia, the Australian Public Sector (APS) was made up of some 100 separate agencies and it employed around 130,000 people. These agencies which comprised both departments of state and statutory bodies varied substantially in size, with the four largest Departments (Social Security; Defence; Employment and Education and Training and Youth Affairs) and the Australian Tax Office accounting for over half of all APS employment.

Prior to the 1990s employees in the APS were covered by a service-wide pay and grading structure supported by common conditions of service throughout the APS. By the end of the 1980s over 130 industrial awards regulated the terms and conditions of service of employees in the APS. The industrial awards specified actual, rather than minimum, rates of pay and conditions of service and were highly prescriptive with respect to both employee entitlements and the detailed regulation of employment relationships and working conditions. This joint regulation of working arrangements within the APS was to change during the nineteen nineties, first through a move to enterprise bargaining within the framework of the Accord agreed between the Labour Government and Australian Council of Trade Unions (ACTU) in the first two years of the decade and then in the mid nineteen nineties, following the election of the Howard government, with a more concerted move toward devolved pay negotiations.

This chapter analyses the changes in pay levels and structure that resulted from the first of these developments, the move to enterprise bargaining. During this period there was scope for bargaining over pay at the level of the enterprise. The terms of this bargaining were very clearly defined but circumscribed by the terms of service-wide agreements. Agency agreements could alter pay but not job classifications, grading, or some other employment conditions regarded as 'essential' and specified in the service-wide government. Despite substantial diversity in the size of the initial pay settlements that were negotiated at the enterprise level a considerable degree of uniformity of pay settlements eventually emerged due to the 'fold-back' provision of the agreement. This provision ultimately awarded something close to the average pay settlement negotiated at the enterprise level to all those who had not negotiated enterprise agreements. It is therefore perhaps surprising that in the face of this perverse incentive structure quite so many agencies negotiated agreements with their unions. Indeed, by the expiry of the first enterprise bargaining agreement agencies employing around 90 per cent of APS staff had negotiated agreements.

The subsequent move, in the mid nineties, to devolved pay negotiations sought to overcome some of the deficiencies and contradictions inherent in the earlier policy and was part of a more general reform package outlined in *Towards a Best Practice Australian Public Service* (Reith, 1996). It proposed to abolish the redistribution of the gains from productivity improvements – the fold-back provision that had been a feature of the previous policy – 4 and to allow greater flexibility in job classification structure at the agency level. It thus abolished most of the key features of the service-wide agreement that had provided the framework for local negotiations under the previous policy.[1]

Private Sector Wage Determination[2]

Until the late nineteen eighties the Australian system of wage determination was highly centralised and in many respects unique. In both the public and private sector, *minimum* rates of pay for industries and occupations covering around 80 per cent of all employees were established in a series of awards made by arbitration and conciliation tribunals. The rates were set by either collective bargaining or arbitration following argument and representation by employers and trade unions.[3] The system had its roots in the early years of the twentieth century when a 'basic wage' or rate of pay judged necessary to keep an unskilled man and his family in a 'civilised' manner was established. A margin for skill was then added to the basic wage with the margin varying from industry to industry. The basic wage was either adjusted in line with the retail price index, or periodically through national wage cases, according to some judgment of the capacity of the economy to sustain a real wage increase. After 1967 the distinction between the basic wage and the skill margin was discontinued and changes in the total wage for employees covered by industrial awards resulted from a series of national wage decisions. Through the early 1970s and 1980s, wage increases also emerged from collective bargaining at industry or enterprise levels which, together with centrally determined pay increases, created the conditions for excessive rates of earnings growth and high levels of industrial disputation.

---

[1] A very informative and comprehensive description and analysis of the policy and of the strengths and weaknesses of the previous policy from an employer perspective is provided in Yates (1998).

[2] For a detailed description of the Australian system of wage setting see Deery and Plowman (1991).

[3] We saw earlier in Tables 1.1 and 1.2 that while in 1990 overall union density was 40 per cent, 98 per cent of public sector employees and 72 per cent of private sector employees were covered by collective bargaining.

In early 1983, a Prices and Incomes Accord was reached by the Australian Labour Party and Australian Council of Trade Unions, which became policy upon the election of the Labour Party to government in March of that year. The Accord was a response to the wage explosion of the preceding years which followed the ending of the regular indexation of award wages in 1981 and the imposition of a wage freeze by the industrial tribunals. The Accord went through a number of phases with an early resumption of indexation, but it was the Accord Mark III which marked the move away from the centralised approach to wage determination in Australia.

The Accord Mark III involved a two-stage wage increase. The first stage of the award was, as before, an across-the-board increase extended to all workers covered by each award. However, a case had to be made for a second stage wage increase which was to be awarded for restructuring and efficiency. By focusing on these issues (particularly restructuring work and management practices), it focused attention on the behaviour of the different enterprises which comprised each industry and became the first step on the road which ultimately led to the proposals for enterprise bargaining. Importantly these second stage, or 'second tier', increases were scrutinised by the Australian Industrial Relations Commission (AIRC) to determine whether they were in the public interest, that is to see whether they represented a genuine productivity increases. The Accords Mark IV and V which operated between 1988 and 1991 involved conditional wage increases, with the criteria for granting the increase being linked to the reform of industrial awards and the removal of instability in award wage relationships.

The Accord Mark VI, introduced in 1991 switched the focus firmly toward enterprise bargaining, although the AIRC was initially reluctant to accept the shift due to concerns about a build up of wage pressures. However, provision was eventually made for unions to negotiate their wage increases at the level of the enterprise, where the emphasis in negotiations would be on improvements in working practices and productivity. Greater emphasis was given to parties reaching agreements which would be registered with the AIRC, a shift backed up by a series of legislative reforms.

The substantial change in the focus of bargaining that occurred at the start of the 1990s should not obscure the fact that even before the introduction of the Accord there was some enterprise bargaining in Australia. Wage drift resulting from 'over-award' payments and even pay settlements in certain sectors was a feature of the Australia system of wage determination prior to the Accord. Studies conducted during the seventies and eighties persistently revealed substantial 'over award' payments in certain sectors and industries which appeared to be explained by a mixture of institutional and market forces, among which the most important were the power of trade unions, firms' profitability and labour demand, (Brown and Fuller, 1978 and Plowman, 1986). The balance between a highly centralised system of bargaining and one with some element of decentralisation appears to have waxed and waned throughout the period.

Evidence on earnings inequality in Australia seems to confirm the picture of a largely centralised system. Movement toward decentralised bargaining is associated with greater earnings inequality (see for example, Metcalf *et al.*, 2000 for the UK and Blau and Kahn, 1996 for international evidence) but in Australia there appears to have been only a small change in earnings inequality during the eighties. Chapter 1 revealed that the dispersion of gross weekly earnings increased quite modestly between 1979 and 1990, with earnings at the highest decile expressed as a percentage of those at the lowest decile increasing by only 2 percentage points (see Table 1.4 earlier). This same study by the OECD (1996) also reveals only a modest widening over the extended period 1980 to 1995 with most of this occurring after 1990. Borland (1996) taking three-year averages to analyse the complete period from July 1975 to May 1993 confirms that, at least for men, most of the widening occurred in the last part of this period (from 1989 onwards). Australia experienced only a modest increase in earnings inequality over the twenty years to 1995. The increase in inequality is substantially less than that in the UK at this time and took place at the end of the period. It should be noted that these same studies reveal that that the degree of earnings inequality was considerably less in Australia than in the UK by the end of the period to 1995.

Public Sector Wage Structure

There has been no detailed analysis of the wage structure in the APS, and until recently there were no studies of the public-private pay differential in Australia. However, the nineteen nineties have seen a number of studies on this latter topic. In 1996, the Australian Public Service and Merit Protection Commission (PSMPC) produced two studies which analyse the growth and distribution of public and private sector average gross weekly earnings over the period 1983 to 1995. The studies conclude that 'the data strongly suggest that the [raw] differentials between earnings in the Commonwealth, State, local government and private sectors are largely a reflection of the skill levels of each' (PSMPC, 1996 and Smith, 1996).

However, the results of these two studies must be treated with caution for they do not distinguish, and therefore cannot control for, some important differences in the composition and productive characteristics of the workforces in the public and private sectors which can account for differences in earnings. It is interesting therefore to look at the few studies which attempt to address this issue.

A study of young people aged between 15 and 26 using data from the 1985 Australian Longitudinal Survey (Vella, 1993) found that government employees among this group earned significantly more than their private sector counterparts. While the introduction of occupational controls, to allow for the heterogeneity of the workforce in the two sectors, reduced the scale of this overpayment, it did not eliminate it. Evidence suggesting a wage premium in the public sector also resulted from a study of union wage premia in Australia. Kornfeld (1993), using the Australian Longitudinal Survey for the years 1984–

1988, concluded that Australian public sector unions raised the wages of all public sector employees but raised the wages of only some private employees.

However, much the most detailed study to date Borland *et al.* (1998) concluded that differences in the average characteristics of employees and jobs in the two sectors fully explained differences in average earnings between the public and private sectors. Employing data from the 1993 Training and Education Experience Survey, they found that when the analysis was conducted at the level of broad occupational group, the one digit level occupational classification, the average weekly earnings of both male and female public sector employees were significantly greater than those of corresponding private sector workers. However, once they controlled for differences in the type of jobs done in the public and private sectors and for differences in the productive characteristics of employees in the two sectors they found most, if not all, of the differential was explained.

Thus, there appears to be very little evidence of any systematic difference in mean wages between the public and private sectors as a whole. However, research has yet to reveal whether there is any difference in the distribution of wages between the two sectors, for in other countries it has been shown that while there may be little difference in mean wages between the two sectors, there is evidence of public sector overpayment at the bottom of the skill and productivity distribution and underpayment at the top of the distribution. This issue awaits further research.

Developments in Central Government Wage Determination

The ground work for the reform of APS bargaining structure can be seen to have been laid as far back as 1984. In that year, the implementation of the proposals laid out in the 1983 White Paper, *Reforming the Australian Public Service*, resulted in the devolution of the operation of personnel management to agencies. This same year saw the introduction of the Financial Management Improvement Programme which contained a range of improvements in resource management. The most significant of these was the Running Cost System which saw the consolidation of salary and administration into a single appropriation and the possibility of borrowing against next year's allocation or carrying over unspent amounts. The devolution of both responsibilities for personnel management and decisions over resource allocation were important preconditions for a move to decentralised wage bargaining.

Prior to 1992, the pay of federal government employees was adjusted in line with national wage decisions by the AIRC for the general economy. In the 1950s and 1960s, periodic adjustment also occurred in line with changes in the market rates of pay of a defined group of occupations in other sectors, while in the seventies this system was supplanted by one of indexation. Uniform pay and grading structures and other conditions of service applied to all those working in organisations covered by the Public Service Act. In the 1950s and 1960s this covered over 70 per cent of all federal government employees, but during the 1970s and 1980s government agencies were increasingly removed from the coverage of the Act so that by the early 1990s, less than 40 per cent were covered.

In 1990 the federal government, responding to the establishment of the Accord Mark VI, which favoured the introduction of enterprise bargaining into the private and public sectors, commissioned a report to assist in developing arrangements for workplace bargaining in the APS. The report (Niland *et al* 1991), complementing work being undertaken by a Committee of Secretaries, contributed to a proposed framework for workplace bargaining with public sector unions in the APS. The resulting industrial agreement, concluded in December 1992, established the basis for enterprise bargaining in federal government departments and agencies. Critically, an integrated public service was to be maintained while allowing for decentralised negotiations on productivity based pay or improvements in working conditions to apply on top of a common pay and grading structure.

The 1992–1994 APS Framework Agreement provided a 'first tier' of Service-wide pay increases. Any pay increases in excess of the service-wide increase which resulted from a 'second tier' of agency-level agreement, had to be funded from productivity and efficiency improvements within the agency. Agreements at the agency level locked bargaining over pay and working practices together, since there could be no pay increases above the service-wide increases without substantial changes in working practices and arrangements. In addition to efficiency savings turning into pay increases, agencies were also required to pay a portion of the efficiency gains into a pool which could be redistributed across the APS to even out pay outcomes between agencies.

The mechanisms established in the Framework Agreement are detailed in Diagram 3.1. The top four 'balloons' represent the types of pay increases available under the Framework Agreement. The final 'balloon', 'Agency Productivity Pay and Conditions', was to be negotiated through Agency Agreements. Agencies could use 50 per cent of the proceeds from increases in efficiency and productivity and up to 15 per cent of revenue increases or program savings (if applicable) flowing from initiatives achieved under their agreements to fund pay increases and improved employment conditions. The other 50 per cent of the efficiency proceeds and at least 85 per cent of the revenue increase or program savings had to be paid back to the Budget. The efficiency proceeds were paid into a 'Foldback' pool to support a pay increase for those who could not achieve efficiency savings within their agency. Thus a 'Foldback Pay Increase' (Balloon 3), could be paid to even out pay differences between agencies if the Foldback Pool was large enough. As it turned out, those who did not earn an equivalent, negotiated increase in their agency agreements had their wages increased by a further 4 per cent by the Foldback increase.[4] The result was that *all* workers in the APS received a 4 per cent increase in wages due to productivity increases and efficiency savings from agencies which negotiated agreements between 1993 and April 1995.

---

[4] This affected approximately 20 per cent of APS workers for the rest of the APS workers had an increase in pay that was stipulated in their Agency Agreements.

Types of pay increase available

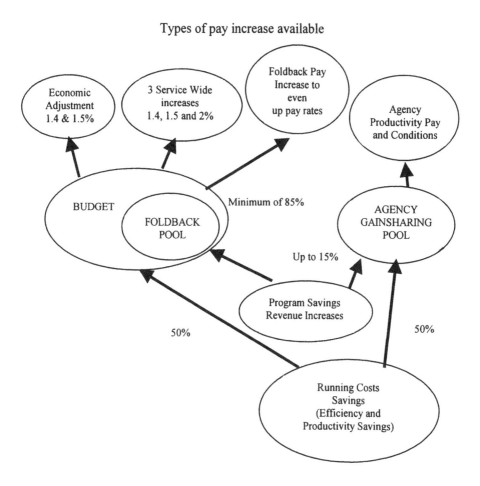

Figure 3.1 Funding of APS Pay Increases Under Agency Bargaining

Source: Adapted from Public Service Union (1995)

Clearly, the incentives of this system were perverse. The policy produced a uniform service-wide increase of 4 per cent with both those who had achieved efficiency savings receiving the same increase and those who had not. The concession of a Foldback increase was offered in the first place to win agreement with the Trade Unions and the expectations were that the size of the Foldback pool would only be sufficient to offer a Foldback increase of around 1 per cent. In the event the size of the pool and the consequent increase came as an unwelcome surprise for it served to undermine the purpose of the original agreement.

Following the 1992–94 Agreement an interim agreement was negotiated. A change of administration had occurred in March 1993 with the return of the

Labour government and the Keating Administration. The Interim Framework Agreement for the APS operated until the end of July 1995 to give effect to the evening-up of base rates of pay across the APS, funded from the Foldback Pool. This was followed by a further Agreement running through to the end of 1996 which reverted to service-wide pay increases based on a Service-wide strategy for Continuous Improvement. The election of a conservative government in early 1996 saw the passing of a new Workplace Relations Act in late 1996, which strongly favoured decentralised bargaining in the community generally with the result that in the APS, agency level agreement negotiations replaced any further Service-wide agreements.

The Incidence of Agency Agreements

By the end of 1995, a time beyond the end of the first phase of workplace bargaining in the APS, 55 APS Agency agreements covering 64 different APS agencies and 88 per cent of the APS staff had been certified. Appendix 3.1 details the timing and the size of the increases in pay negotiated in the APS from 1991 to 1996. The agreements in bold represent Service-wide increases, while the agreements in normal type are the pay increases that were bargained at the agency level. The December 1992 Service-wide increase of 2 per cent was linked to general productivity measures and was only temporarily funded from the budget. The March 1993 and 1994 Service-wide increases of 1.4 and 1.5 per cent, respectively, were stipulated in the 1992–1994 Framework Agreement and were funded out of the budget. The other increases, except the Foldback adjustments of January, April and June 1995, were negotiated at the agency level and were funded from productivity and efficiency increases. Most of the increases applied to all staff below the Senior Executive level, with the Senior Officer Grade (SOG) classifications also often having the option to have their pay augmented by performance based pay increases. Many of the increases were moderate (between 1 and 2 per cent) although over the two years (through December 1995) several larger agencies had negotiated increases of between 3 and 4 per cent. However, overall the dispersion in the size of pay increases that were negotiated at the agency level was modest and since the duration of agency bargaining was no more than two years, there was little opportunity for substantial differences in pay between employees in different agencies to emerge.

    The 1994–95 APS Interim Agreement specified the levels of the Foldback increases that removed the dispersion in pay outcomes that emerged from 1992–94. The 1995–96 APS Agreement specified Service-wide pay increases only, in three steps of 2 per cent in July 1995, 1.6 per cent in March 1996 and 2 per cent in October 1996. (It precluded agency level pay negotiations.) In total, when service-wide and agency increases are taken together over the period from December 1992 to October 1996, APS employees realised an increase in their incomes of 14.5 per cent, 4 per cent of which was derived from agency level productivity savings achieved by agencies and redistributed across the Service.

Improvements in some working conditions were also negotiated in agency agreements. Leave provisions, to cover provisions for family or carers leave and parental leave, were introduced. Almost 85 per cent of agreements made or adjusted provision for carers leave and/or sick leave. Other negotiated changes involved more flexible hours arrangements and an increase in the number of hours that might be worked per day before overtime payments began. Fifty-five per cent of agreements encouraged part-time employment but this was severely qualified in most agreements for this was only to be on a permanent basis. Many agencies' agreements specified that employment should be focused on the 'ongoing workforce' (49 per cent of agreements) and only a small number of agreements reserved the right to hire contract labour or other forms of temporary employment. Despite these evident limitations, the overall savings achieved by the 1992–94 Agreement were judged sufficient to warrant a 4 per cent fold back increase.

Motivation for Reform

In 1991 the Australian Industrial Relations Commission (AIRC) rejected the argument that the prevailing version of the Accord should promote a greater incidence of enterprise bargaining. This judgment was heavily criticised by both the federal government of the day and the Australian Council of Trade Unions. It prompted the federal government to issue its own guidelines for reform and to use its position as a major employer to promote decentralised bargaining. In May of that year, agreement was reached with public sector unions on a framework for workplace bargaining,[5] and in October, the AIRC relented in its opposition to workplace bargaining and permitted parties to make their own arrangements for bargaining at this level.

Fundamental to the push to workplace bargaining on the part of the federal government was the conviction that the reform of industrial relations was the key to improved productivity and international competitiveness and that the necessary improvements in industrial relations could not be delivered by the old centralised bargaining arrangements. The AIRC was concerned about the repeat of earlier wage explosions under less centralised wage arrangements and saw workplace bargaining as a threat to its existence. It is therefore, perhaps, not surprising that the AIRC initially rejected the idea that it should promote workplace bargaining.

The arguments for workplace bargaining in the APS were similar to those advanced in other countries. It was recognised that the APS produced a considerable variety of different services for the public and that each different line of service delivery required its own mix of different skills, working patterns and arrangements. What was described as 'an extensive and well-defined management structure' offered, it seemed, the opportunity to decentralise decisions over pay and conditions and to identify opportunities to improve performance at a local level.

---

[5] See *Improving Productivity: A Challenge for the APS*, Department of Industrial Relations, 1991.

Yet a critical feature of workplace bargaining in Australia was to be the retention of a centralised grading structure, with the objective of ensuring a service wide career structure for APS personnel. This aspect above all others distinguished the Australian from the Swedish and UK forms of decentralised bargaining, that were introduced at the same time.

Analysis of APS Pay

Chapter 2 reported that the data for the Australian APS focuses on full-time employees in the years 1990 and 1996, years before and after the first rounds of enterprise bargaining. Chapter 2 also provided an initial description of some of the properties of this data, detailing in Table 2.4 the distribution of APS employees by region and agency and the gender composition, average age and period in government service of the work force. It also reported the educational composition of the workforce, the real pay levels of employees in the APS in 1990 and 1996 and distinguished the gender pay gap in each of these years.

In this section, we examine pay in the APS in greater detail. First, we examine changes in real median earnings for the complete sample, and for the major grades and eight largest departments in the APS. Taken together, these eight agencies accounted for 80 per cent of employment in the APS in 1996. We further analyse these changes by gender. Second, we analyse pay dispersion using three measures of dispersion: the standard deviation, the ratio of pay at the first decile to pay at the median and ratio of pay at the ninth decile to pay at the median. Next we report the results of the OLS estimations, in order to distinguish changes in the composition and pay structure of the APS workforce. We analyse the changes in the pay structure that resulted from the reforms, focusing on by state, and by department and agency. Finally, we decompose the changes in pay in order to reveal the relative impact of changes in composition and changes in the pay structure on the growth in pay in the APS over this period.

Pay Growth and Dispersion by Grade and Agency or Department

In Table 3.1, we report real median pay growth over the period, 1990 to 1996, for each of the main grades and the largest departments in the APS. The median pay of all employees in the APS grew in real terms by 17.5 per cent over the period 1990 to 1996 (see also Table 2.4). However, there is considerable variation around this rate of increase. The rates of pay of some grades increased substantially faster than others and employees in some departments received much greater increases in pay than others.

The real median pay of women increased faster than that of men (as Table 2.4 also revealed), and the rate of growth of pay for women exceeded that for men by the largest amount in the grade in which a majority of women are employed, ASOs. For the highest level grades there were no gender differences in growth rates. On the other hand in the two lowest grades, General Service Officers and Other

Grades, the median pay of women advanced less rapidly than that of men. There was an even greater difference between the experience of men and women at the level of the eight largest agencies and departments shown in Table 3.1. In each of the agencies the pay of women increased faster than that of men. The increases for women ranged from a high of 32.1 per cent for women in Veteran Affairs to a low of 16.3 per cent for women in Employment, Education, and Youth Training Affairs. The increase for men was greatest in Foreign Affairs and Trade (16.7 per cent) and smallest in Social Security (6.4 per cent). The department with the greatest differences between the rates of growth of real median pay for men and women was Social Security.

Table 3.1, therefore establishes, first that in every department the median pay of women increased faster than that of men but that; second, this is not true of all of the main grades and that third; the faster increase in women's pay overall seems to have resulted from the much faster growth in pay in the ASO grade which is numerically the most important grade for women. Finally, Table 3.1 has established that there are substantial differences in the pace of real pay growth between departments and grades.

A very similar picture of substantial variation in the experience of real pay growth of different grades and departments emerges from an analysis of the changes in the dispersion of pay which are detailed in Table 3.2. This table reports substantial variation in both the levels of and changes in the dispersion of pay between the genders and between the different grades and departments.

In the APS as a whole pay dispersion changed very little over the six years to 1996. The standard deviation, one measure of dispersion, fell from 0.33 to 0.30 between 1990 and 1996. However, the 90/10 ratio, which can be computed by dividing the 90/50 ratio shown in Table 3.2 by the 10/50 ratio shown in the same table, was unchanged at 2.10 in both 1990 and 1996. This stability was due to two offsetting developments again evident in Table 3.2. First there was a widening in pay differentials at the top of the pay distribution; but second there was a marked improvement in the relative pay of low paid workers in the APS. The 10/50 percentile ratio narrowed from 0.67 to 0.72 while the 90/50 percentile widened from 1.41 to 1.51.

The experience of men and women was again quite different. The standard deviation suggests that both pay distributions narrowed over the period. However, the 90/10 ratios suggest otherwise. The male distribution exhibits a sharp increase in the relative pay of those at the top decile from 1.34 in 1990 to 1.60 in 1996 and although this is offset by a narrowing of the 50/10 ratio, as the position of the lowest paid males improves, from 0.62 to 0.73, overall the 90/10 ratio widens from 2.16 in 1990 to 2.19 in 1996. Women, at both the 90th and the 10th percentile experienced a decline in their relative pay, the former fell from 1.53 to 1.48 and the latter from 0.76 to 0.71. However, the impact of the latter clearly dominated because the overall dispersion widened: the 90/10 ratio widened from 2.01 in 1990 to 2.08 in 1996.

Women's pay is slightly less dispersed than that of men. In the extreme case, GSO's in 1990, the dispersion of pay among men as measured by the standard deviation is twice as large as that for women. There is rather more variation in the 90/50 ratio for men than for women while the 10/50 ratios are very similar.

There are also substantial differences between the dispersion of pay in the eight agencies. In 1996 pay was least dispersed in Employment, Education and Youth Training Affairs, with a standard deviation of 0.24 for all employees in 1996 and most dispersed in Foreign Affairs and Trade, with a standard deviation of 0.33 in the same year. Again the standard deviation measure hides important differences between men and women. In the lower half of the distribution of pay, as measured by the 10/50 ratio, pay is less dispersed among women than among men. In the upper half however, the reverse is the case, pay dispersion, as measured by the 90/50 ratio, appears to be greater among men.

What accounts for the growth in pay observed in Table 3.1? The size of pay settlements is one explanation. In addition most employees in the APS were paid on incremental scales and therefore movements up these pay scales, will have boosted the pay of some employees. Appendix 3.1 reported the pay settlements received by APS employees between 1991 and 1996. However, the table revealed that there was only modest variation in the size of settlements received as a result of agency bargaining between 1994 and 1996. Moreover, the foldback increases awarded to those who failed to conclude agency agreements further reduced the variation in settlement size. Table 3.1 revealed considerable variation in the average rates of pay growth between different grades and departments and it seems unlikely this can be accounted for by the above two factors. Changes in the composition of the workforce in the different agencies and grades may account for some of the changes that occurred. Reducing the proportion staff in particular grades or increasing the skills required of new entrants would change the composition of the workforce and would be associated with increases in pay that would be different from the increases detailed in the APS Agreements. The raw data confounds the effects of changes in workforce composition and changes in the pay structure on pay growth. The changing composition of the workforce in some departments may have an effect on pay growth which is greater than the effects of the uniform pay settlement. Where the relevant characteristics of the workforce can be measured, regression analysis can be used to distinguish the impact of changes on workforce composition on pay growth. Where other important features of the APS pay structure can also be included in the regression analysis it will distinguish the impact of these on the pay of APS employees.

Table 3.1 Real Median Monthly Pay by Grade and Department in the Australian APS in 1990 and 1996

(in 1990 prices, A$s)	All Employees			Females			Males		
	1990	1996	% Change	1990	1996	% Change	1990	1996	% Change
All Employees	2496.17	2932.61	17.5	2088.33	2692.28	28.9	2827.50	2987.11	5.6
GRADES									
Senior Executives	5169.84	5826.91	12.7	5169.84	5826.91	12.7	5169.84	5826.91	12.7
Senior Officers	3527.25	3977.71	12.8	3527.25	3977.71	12.8	3527.25	3977.71	12.8
ASO's	2256.67	2692.28	19.3	1985.83	2401.20	20.9	2530.83	2692.28	6.4
General Service Officers	1725.00	1953.33	13.2	1599.83	1748.45	9.3	1808.17	2019.89	11.7
Other Grades, nec	2883.92	3163.68	9.7	2801.92	2922.24	4.3	2926.92	3338.19	14.1
AGENCIES-DEPARTMENTS									
Defence	2335.58	2922.24	25.1	1935.00	2340.53	21.0	2709.50	2985.27	10.2
Veteran Affairs	2315.00	2932.61	26.7	2037.50	2692.28	32.1	2595.83	2932.61	13.0
Employment, Education, etc	2390.83	2765.67	15.7	2315.00	2692.28	16.3	2595.83	2932.61	13.0
Foreign, Affairs And Trade	3032.50	3977.71	31.2	2466.67	3145.29	27.5	3408.83	3977.71	16.7
Social Security	2088.33	2692.28	28.9	1847.17	2401.20	30.0	2530.83	2692.28	6.4
Customs	2358.67	2762.44	17.1	2088.33	2446.28	17.1	2645.83	2820.01	6.6
Australian Tax Office	2315.00	2852.30	23.2	2037.50	2479.60	21.7	2750.00	3061.38	11.3
Administrative Services	2827.50	3338.19	18.8	2256.67	2932.61	30.0	2951.67	3431.30	16.2

Table 3.2 Pay Dispersion by Grade and Department in the Australian APS in 1990 and 1996

(in 1990 A$s)	All Employees						Females						Males					
	Standard Deviations		10/50		90/50		Standard Deviations		10/50		90/50		Standard Deviations		10/50		90/50	
	1990	1996	1990	1996	1990	1996	1990	1996	1990	1996	1990	1996	1990	1996	1990	1996	1990	1996
Full Sample	0.33	0.30	0.67	0.72	1.41	1.51	0.28	0.27	0.76	0.71	1.53	1.48	0.32	0.29	0.62	0.73	1.34	1.60
GRADES																		
Senior Executives	0.12	0.13	0.90	1.0	1.21	1.23	0.09	0.12	0.90	0.96	1.11	1.23	0.12	0.13	0.90	1.0	1.21	1.23
Senior Officers	0.11	0.12	0.97	1.0	1.16	1.20	0.12	0.15	0.97	1.01	1.16	1.20	0.11	0.10	0.97	1.0	1.16	1.20
ASO	0.25	0.21	0.72	0.73	1.41	1.27	0.23	0.21	0.80	0.79	1.42	1.31	0.24	0.20	0.66	0.79	1.31	1.27
General Service Officers	0.21	0.23	0.92	0.85	1.50	1.58	0.10	0.14	0.97	0.92	1.13	1.21	0.21	0.23	0.88	0.87	1.58	1.45
Other Grades, nec	0.35	0.29	0.73	0.70	1.36	1.51	0.35	0.31	0.70	0.68	1.31	1.51	0.35	0.28	0.73	0.72	1.37	1.43
AGENCIES-DEPARTMENTS																		
Defence	0.32	0.32	0.70	0.65	1.55	1.63	0.25	0.27	0.81	0.78	1.47	1.47	0.31	0.32	0.63	0.65	1.41	1.60
Veteran Affairs	0.34	0.30	0.69	0.65	1.52	1.36	0.29	0.30	0.78	0.71	1.56	1.48	0.37	0.29	0.63	0.74	1.58	1.63
Employment, Education, etc	0.26	0.24	0.72	0.83	1.43	1.44	0.25	0.23	0.70	0.85	1.38	1.48	0.24	0.23	0.71	0.82	1.36	1.36
Foreign Affairs and Trade	0.33	0.33	0.67	0.67	1.42	1.47	0.27	0.31	0.86	0.81	1.64	1.76	0.31	0.31	0.63	0.62	1.56	1.47
Social Security	0.27	0.26	0.76	0.71	1.49	1.27	0.25	0.25	0.85	0.79	1.53	1.38	0.28	0.27	0.64	0.71	1.31	1.48
Customs	0.53	0.26	0.73	0.72	1.40	1.45	0.42	0.27	0.76	0.81	1.38	1.40	0.57	0.25	0.73	0.78	1.33	1.41
Australian Tax Office	0.30	0.27	0.70	0.76	1.52	1.40	0.24	0.24	0.78	0.83	1.49	1.38	0.30	0.27	0.59	0.71	1.28	1.56
Administrative Services	0.27	0.28	0.67	0.72	1.36	1.43	0.26	0.29	0.76	0.74	1.47	1.43	0.24	0.26	0.71	0.74	1.36	1.39

Regression Results

The results of the OLS estimates of the determinants of pay in the APS in 1990 and 1996 are reported in Table 3.3. The results are taken from the 'country specific' specification which employs the full range of variables available for Australia which are unique among the three countries studied, and also includes a measure of education. It also identifies all the major agencies within the APS and therefore allows for detailed analysis of the inter-agency pay structure. It will be seen in Chapter 6 that much less detailed reporting of agency affiliation is available in the 'common specification' for this includes only those variables available for all three countries. However, it is used only in the analysis in Chapter 6. The OLS estimates reported in Table 3.3 distinguish the effects on pay of the employees age, their education and years of government service as well as the effects on pay of the grade of the employee, the department or agency in which they work and the region in which they work. All of the coefficients shown in Table 3.3 are significant at the 1 per cent level except where indicated by either an 'a' or 'b'.

As employees grow older, they generally become more experienced and productive and this is one of the reasons why pay generally tends to rise with age. Table 3.3 reveals that this is also true in the APS. However, as elsewhere, the addition to pay associated with age is shown to diminish, this is revealed by the negative sign of the squared age term. In 1990 the age at which maximum pay was attained for women was 40 while in that same year it was attained at age 46 for men. By 1996 the age of maximum earnings had risen to 44 years for women but had remained constant at 46 for men.

The regression controls for the effect of the employees grade on their pay so it controls for the fact that more men than women are found in the higher grades of the APS. However, it cannot control for the fact that within each of the grades shown, men may fill more of the senior and better-paid posts. These posts will be filled through promotion and it is likely to be older employees who gain promotion. This is likely to be the explanation for the results shown here. Men occupy more of the senior posts within each grade and they tend to be older than the average in the grade. The higher age of peak pay for men reflects this fact, although it is noteworthy that women are catching up rapidly.

The regression results also show how pay rises with age in the years before men and women in the APS achieve their maximum pay. This is done in the following way. First, we differentiate equation (1) from Chapter 2 with respect to the AGE variable. Setting the resulting derivative equal to zero and solving for AGE gives us the age at which earnings are maximised. In general terms, this results in the following equation:

$$AGE^* = \frac{-\hat{\beta}^{AGE}}{2\hat{\beta}^{AGESQ}} \qquad (1)$$

where AGE* is the age where earnings are maximised and the $\hat{\beta}^{AGE}$ and $\hat{\beta}^{AGESQ}$ are the estimated coefficients for AGE and AGESQ, respectively.

Table 3.3 Regression Results for 1990 and 1996 – Australia

	1990			1996		
Variable	All Employees	Female	Male	All Employees	Female	Male
	(1)	(2)	(3)	(4)	(5)	(6)
Constant	7.690	7.662	7.708	7.938	8.021	7.889
Male	0.040			0.036		
Tengov	0.034	0.042	0.031	0.023	0.022	0.023
Tengovso	-7.1E-4	-1.0E-3	-6.2E-4	-3.8E-4	-3.7E-4	-3.8E-4
Age	0.020	0.023	0.021	0.019	0.017	0.023
Ageso	-2.3E-4	-2.9E-4	-2.3E-4	-2.1E-4	-1.9E-4	-2.5E-4
ED1	0.068	0.063	0.073	0.056	0.056	0.058
ED2	0.130	0.127	0.128	0.086	0.091	0.083
ED3	0.192	0.183	0.193	0.148	0.127	0.158
STATE						
New S. Wales	-0.095	-0.083	-0.104	-0.090	-0.081	-0.097
Victoria	-0.101	-0.096	-0.103	-0.090	-0.096	-0.087
Queensland	-0.107	-0.097	-0.114	-0.097	-0.089	-0.102
S. Australia	-0.099	-0.100	-0.099	-0.079	-0.080	-0.080
W. Australia	-0.134	-0.107	-0.152	-0.095	-0.098	-0.092
Tasmania	-0.110	-0.109	-0.108	-0.093	-0.080	-0.100
N. Territories	-0.051	-0.041	-0.054	-0.045	-0.030	-0.059
DEPARTMENT/AGENCY						
AIPO	-0.142	-0.096	-0.167	-0.115	-0.106	-0.124
ACCC	-0.058	-0.059	-0.059	-0.133	-0.178	-0.086
PSMPRA	-0.066	-0.082	-0.052	-0.082	-0.056	-0.113
AIDAB	-0.055	-0.012	-0.081	-0.081	-0.015	-0.124
AGPS	-0.089	-0.081	-0.097	-0.101	-0.067	-0.119
ATSIC	0.029	0.031	0.022[a]	-0.011[a]	0.011[a]	-0.036
AWM	-0.091	-0.061	-0.126	-0.105	-0.049[a]	-0.138
NCA	0.031	-0.007[a]	0.076	0.054	0.023[a]	0.084
AGSO	-0.124	-0.151	-0.126	-0.023	-0.036[a]	-0.036
NLA	-0.194	-0.186	-0.190	-0.149	-0.131	-0.156
PMC	-0.035	-0.011[a]	-0.061	-0.067	-0.045	-0.092
ANAO	0.004[a]	0.023[a]	-0.009[a]	-0.070	-0.067	-0.078
DVA	-0.058	-0.053	-0.061	-0.086	-0.067	-0.102
WEATHER	-0.115	-0.081	-0.124	-0.097	-0.044	-0.116
AEC	0.002[a]	0.011[a]	-0.004[a]	-0.049	-0.052	-0.054

Table 3.3 (Contd.)

Variable	1990			1996		
	All Employees	Female	Male	All Employees	Female	Male
DSS	-0.086	-0.085	-0.092	-0.082	-0.074	-0.098
Archives	-0.055	-0.019^a	-0.085	-0.113	-0.090	-0.130
Indcom	-0.088	-0.095	-0.082	-0.079	-0.073	-0.087
Treasury	-0.089	-0.100	-0.085	-0.088	-0.043	-0.112
DPP	0.107	0.077	0.132	0.081	0.077	0.090
Comsuper	-0.177	-0.102	-0.123	-0.154	-0.145	-0.158
ABS	-0.084	-0.055	-0.105	-0.111	-0.091	-0.127
Customs	-0.202	-0.170	-0.219	-0.243	-0.243	-0.245
ATO	-0.037	-0.032	-0.044	-0.060	-0.051	-0.069
Defence	-0.083	-0.089	-0.085	-0.088	-0.109	-0.087
Finance	-0.047	-0.028	-0.060	-0.071	-0.057	-0.084
Health	0.074	0.086	0.062	0.076	0.119	0.042
ANCA	-0.068	-0.101	-0.060	-0.084	-0.089	-0.083
DIR	-0.009^a	-0.004^a	-0.019^a	-0.053	-0.042	-0.066
DEETYA	-0.049	-0.038	-0.065	-0.040	-0.014^a	-0.069
DPIE	-0.110	-0.043	-0.134	-0.132	-0.043	-0.165
DFAT	-0.117	-0.108	-0.127	-0.116	-0.110	-0.124
ADMIN	-0.048	-0.050	-0.052	-0.045	-0.033	-0.058
IMMIG	-0.050	-0.032	-0.068	-0.062	-0.035	-0.086
ABARE	-0.095	-0.082	-0.104	-0.126	-0.122	-0.132
ISC	-0.023^a	-0.003^a	-0.041^a	-1.2E-3^a	0.025^a	-0.027
COMCARE	-0.009^a	-0.005^a	-0.018^a	-0.065	-0.056	-0.072
GRADE						
SES	0.574	0.672	0.562	0.720	0.808	0.710
SO	0.283	0.368	0.276	0.429	0.518	0.420
ASO	0.055	0.105	0.059	0.105	0.168	0.106
OTHER	0.232	0.301	0.227	0.307	0.362	0.306
Adjusted R^2	0.627	0.558	0.600	0.656	0.514	0.696

Notes: a.   The omitted variables are: ACT for State; Attorney General for Department/Agency and GSO for grade.

     b.   All coefficients are significant at the 5 per cent level except when indicated with ^{a}, which denotes insignificance at conventional levels.

Using this formula and the estimated results of the AGE and AGESQ coefficients from Table 3.3, we calculate that the age at which earnings were maximised, holding all other variables constant, was 43.9 years in 1990. However, it rose slightly to 45.2 years of age by 1996. There were also some differences by gender in the age at which highest earnings are attained. In 1990 the age of maximum earnings occurred at 39.7 and 45.7 years for women and men, respectively. This gap narrowed to 44.7 and 46.0 years, respectively.

Pay also rises with the length of time spent in government service, but if pay growth had been determined by this factor alone, it would have peaked much earlier than it did as a result of the effects of age; after about 25 years service for men and 20 years for women in 1990.[6] Again, this relationship is shown to have changed by 1996 with earnings at a maximum after 29 years of service for men and women. The proximate explanation for the positive association between pay and years of government service is that it reflects the impact of the incremental scales employed throughout the APS at this time, as well as any promotions occurring *within* the grades distinguished in the analysis. The more fundamental reason however, is that employees are rewarded for their increased productivity as a result of increased experience and sector specific skills and these grow with age and length of time in government service. Note that Table 3.3 suggests that these effects have diminished over the period studied.

Pay also rises with education. In 1990 employees with secondary school qualifications only, ED1, received a salary which was on average 7.0 per cent higher than received by staff with 'low or no qualifications', the omitted category. The mark-ups over those with 'low or no qualifications' of the same gender were 6.5 per cent for women and 7.6 per cent for men.[7] Those staff with some post-secondary school qualifications, ED2, received salaries which were on average 13.9 per cent higher than those with 'low or no qualifications' while those with a university degree, ED3, received 21.2 per cent more. The respective additions for women and men were 13.5 and 13.7 per cent at ED2 and 20.1 and 21.3 per cent at ED3. These additions to pay were of course those additions identified after controlling for the independent effects of the individual's grade on their pay.

By 1996 the more highly educated still received more pay than those with 'low or no qualifications' but the returns had diminished. The mark-ups of all employees on the pay of those with low or no qualifications were now 5.8, 9.0 and 16.0 per cent for ED1, ED2 and ED3, respectively which were down from the 7.0, 13.9 and 21.2, respectively, in 1990 shown above. The returns to education, the additional pay received by those with the highest educational qualifications, in the APS therefore declined substantially over the period.

---

[6] The methodology used here is the same as for finding the age where earnings are maximised. The general formula for this is:

$$TENGOV* = \frac{-\hat{\beta}^{TENGOV}}{2\hat{\beta}^{TENGOVSQ}} \qquad (2)$$

[7] The percentage mark-up is found by taking the exponent of the coefficient subtracting 1 from the result and multiplying by 100, that is [exp (coefficient)-1]x100.

The decline was experienced by both men and women. The percentage mark-ups for women in the APS at ED1, ED2 and ED3 were 5.8, 9.5 and 13.5 in 1996 compared to 6.5, 13.5 and 20.1 respectively in 1990. For men they were 6.0, 8.7 and 17.1 in 1996 at ED1, ED2 and ED3 respectively compared to 7.6, 13.7 and 21.3 respectively in 1990. This sizeable fall in the returns in education in the APS over this period seems likely to reflect the increasing proportion of APS employees who hold a degree (refer back to Table 2.4) many of whom are now employed in the more junior grades in the APS.

The Inter-State Pay Structure

In most countries there exist differences between the pay in the different regions of the country even after controlling for differences in the industrial, and therefore occupational mix of the workforce, and for differences in the education, gender and age of the workforce in different regions. One of the reasons is that there are differences in the cost of living in different parts of the country and employers find that they have to compensate employees for these differences. Another reason is that some parts of the country are more or less pleasant to work in and therefore there is respectively a greater and lesser supply of labour to these areas. This said, the public sector in most countries, the US excepted, makes less attempt to compensate its employees for regional cost of living differences than does the private sector and it pays its employees on national pay scales. As a general rule we should not therefore expect to find as much regional differentiation in pay in the public sector as we do in the private. However, the move to decentralised bargaining offers the opportunity for greater regional differentiation of pay and to bring public sector rates of pay into line with those in local markets. It is therefore interesting to distinguish whether the move to agency agreements in the APS resulted in greater regional differentiation of pay.

The results are shown in Table 3.4. This table takes the coefficients on the variables which capture the state in which the APS employee works and converts these into percentages. They show the percentage differences in pay between APS workers in the Australian Capital Territories (ACT), the omitted state, and each of the other states after controlling for all of the other differences between employees as measured by all of the other variables in Table 3.3. Table 3.4 shows that in general the regional structure of pay has changed little over the period. The move to agency agreements has not altered the regional pay structure. Those in the ACT received the highest pay, with pay in the ACT typically around 10 per cent greater than in all other states, save one. That one is the Northern Territories where pay was around 5 per cent higher than in any of the other states, except the ACT, in both 1990 and 1996. In the Northern Territories employees in the APS are offered additional pay to induce them to work in this area.

In 1990 there were greater differences in the inter-state pay structures for men than there were for women, but by 1996 these differences had diminished. Just why there should be greater differences in the 'regional' structure of pay for men than for women, once we have controlled for all of the main differences between men and women, is not clear. In the private sector we might expect to observe differences in pay between regions because of higher compensation paid to employees living in high cost areas, but these are likely to be the same for men and women. In the APS such payments are anyway rare.

Table 3.4 The Inter-State Structure of Pay in the APS
(Percentage differences from pay in the ACT)

	1990			1996		
	All Employees	Females	Males	All Employees	Females	Males
	(1)	(2)	(3)	(4)	(5)	(6)
New South Wales	-9.1	-7.9	-9.9	-8.6	-7.8	-9.2
Victoria	-9.6	-9.2	-9.8	-8.6	-9.2	-8.3
Queensland	-10.1	-9.2	-10.8	-9.2	-8.5	-9.7
South Australia	-9.4	-9.5	-9.4	-7.6	-7.7	-7.7
Western Australia	-12.5	-10.1	-14.1	-9.1	-9.3	-8.8
Tasmania	-10.4	-10.3	-10.2	-8.9	-7.7	-9.5
Northern Territories	-5.0	-4.0	-5.3	-4.4	-3.0	-5.7

Notes: a.   Constructed from the coefficients reported in Table 3.3 where the coefficients are converted to percentage differences by: $(\exp(\beta)-1)*100$.

b.   All coefficients are significant at the 5 per cent level.

The Department and Agency Pay Structure

The overall inter-departmental wage structure is revealed by the coefficients reported for each of the agencies in Table 3.5. This again takes the percentage differences in pay between the department or agency of interest and a reference agency, in this case the Attorney General Department, after controlling for the effects on pay of all of the other independent variables recorded in Table 3.3. A number of the agencies reported employ very few staff, and this is one of the reasons why the coefficients are not significant. Where either an 'a' or 'b' is indicated, this reveals that the estimated coefficients in Table 3.3 could not be regarded as significantly different from the reference category and therefore the percentage difference are not statistically significantly different at the 5 per cent level from the Attorney General Department.

For the vast majority of agencies robust results emerge for both 1990 and 1996. Thus the Director of Public Prosecution (DPP) department emerges as the highest paying agency in both 1990 and 1996 with the pay of all employees 11.3 and 8.5 per cent higher in 1990 and 1996 respectively than in the Attorney General's department. At the other end, the lowest paying department in both years was Customs with pay 18.3 and 21.5 per cent lower in 1990 and 1996, respectively than the omitted department. Customs is the lowest paying for both men and women in 1990 and 1996, while Health is the highest paying agency for women in 1990 and 1996 and the DPP is the highest paying for men in both years.

Table 3.5 reveals that there are substantial differences between pay in different departments and agencies even after controlling for differences in the grade structure, and the gender, age and educational composition of their workforces. In 1990 the differences between the average pay in different departments was considerably greater for men than for women. The highest paying department for men in 1990 paid 33.9 per cent more than the lowest while in that same year the highest paying department for women paid only 26.0 per cent more than the lowest. The summary statistic, maximum minus minimum percentage difference shown in Table 3.5, measures the range between the highest and lowest paying departments in each year.

Why should there be such large differences between departments? One explanation is differences in workforce composition differences in the skills and quality of the workforce which are not captured by the variables included in the OLS equations. It is plausible that the five grades into which employees were classified are too broad to capture important differences between some of the more specialised and technical skills deployed by employees in the different departments. Agency bargaining would alter the inter-departmental pay structure, if agencies agreed different sized pay awards for this would cause pay levels in different agencies to begin to diverge. If agencies had also been able to change the grading structure this would have caused further divergence. Yet we noted above that a feature of the move to agency bargaining in the APS was the retention of a service-wide grading structure and we also saw that there was only a modest differentiation in the size of pay awards at the agency level. We would therefore not predict that the move to agency bargaining would have a substantial impact on the inter agency pay structure in Australia. It is therefore interesting to note that there was no reduction in the differences in pay between departments and agencies between 1990 and 1996. Even though agency bargaining should have been better able to identify and compensate these differences we have noted the limited scope that this offered for differentiating pay. It is noteworthy that the difference between the highest and lowest paying department was virtually unchanged at 29.6 per cent in 1990 to 30.0 per cent in 1996. The standard deviation, another measure of dispersion, narrowed only marginally, from 6.1 to 5.8, over this same period.

Table 3.5 The Departmental and Agency Pay Structure in the APS (Percentage Differences in Pay from the Attorney General's Department)

	1990			1996		
	All employees	Females	Males	All employees	Females	Males
	(1)	(2)	(3)	(4)	(5)	(6)
SUMMARY STATISTICS						
Max minus min percentage difference	29.6	26.0	33.9	30.0	34.1	31.3
Standard deviation of percentage difference	6.1	5.7	6.7	5.8	6.1	6.0
DEPARTMENTAL DIFFERENCES						
AIPO	-13.2	-9.1	-15.4	-10.9	-10.0	-11.7
ACCC	-5.6	-5.7	-5.7	-10.6	-16.3	-8.2
PSMPC	-6.3	-7.9	-5.1	-7.9	-5.5	-10.6
AIDAB	-5.3	-1.2	-7.8	-7.8	-1.5	-11.7
AGPS	-8.5	-7.8	-9.2	-9.6	-6.5	-11.2
ATSIC	2.9	3.2	2.2[a]	-1.1[a]	1.1[a]	-3.5
AWM	-8.7	-6.0	-11.9	-10.0	-4.8[a]	-12.9
NCA	3.2	-0.7[a]	7.9	5.6	2.3[a]	8.8
AGSO	-11.6	-14.0	-11.9	-2.3	-3.5[a]	-3.5
NLA	-17.7	-17.0	-17.3	-13.8	-12.2	-14.5
PMC	-3.4	-1.1[a]	-5.9	-6.5	-4.4	-8.8
ANAO	0.4[a]	2.4[a]	-0.9[a]	-6.8	-6.5	-7.5
DVA	-5.6	-5.2	-5.9	-8.3	-6.5	-9.7
WEATHER	-10.9	-7.8	-11.6	-9.3	-4.3	-10.9
AEC	0.2[a]	1.1[a]	-0.4[a]	-4.8	-5.1	-5.3
DSS	-8.3	-8.2	-8.8	-8.1	-7.1	-9.4
ARCHIVES	-5.4	-1.8[a]	-8.1	-10.6	-8.6	-12.2
INDCOM	-8.4	-9.0	-7.9	-7.6	-7.1	-8.4
TREASURY	-8.6	-9.5	-8.1	-8.5	-4.2	-10.6
DPP	11.3	8.0	14.2	8.5	8.0	9.4
COMSUPER	-11.0	-9.7	-11.6	-14.2	-13.5	-14.6
ABS	-8.1	-5.4	-10.0	-10.5	-8.7	-11.9
CUSTOMS	-18.3	-15.6	-19.7	-21.5	-21.5	-21.8
ATO	-3.6	-3.1	-4.3	-5.8	-5.0	-6.7
DEFENCE	-7.9	-8.5	-8.2	-8.4	-10.3	-8.3
FINANCE	-4.6	-2.7	-5.9	-6.9	-5.5	-8.1

Table 3.5 (Contd.)

	1990			1996		
	All employees	Females	Males	All employees	Females	Males
HEALTH	7.7	9.0	6.4	7.9	12.6	4.3
ANCA	-6.6	-9.6	-5.8	-8.1	-8.5	-7.9
DIR	-0.9[a]	-0.4[a]	-1.9[a]	-5.2	-4.1	-6.4
DEETYA	-4.8	-3.7	-6.3	-4.0	-1.3[a]	-6.7
DPIE	-10.4	-4.2	-12.5	-12.4	-4.2	-15.2
DFAT	-11.1	-10.2	-11.9	-10.9	-10.4	-11.7
ADMIN	-4.6	-4.9	-5.1	-4.4	-3.3	-5.6
DIMA	-4.9	-3.2	-6.6	-6.0	-3.4	-8.3
ABARE	-9.0	-7.8	-9.9	-11.8	-11.5	-12.4
ISC	-2.2[a]	-0.3[a]	-4.0[a]	-0.1[a]	2.5[a]	-2.6
COMCARE	-0.9[a]	-0.5[a]	-1.8[a]	-6.3	-5.4	-6.9

Notes: a.   Constructed from the coefficients reported in Table 3.3 where the coefficients have been converted to percentage differences by: $(exp(\beta)-1)*100$.

b.   All coefficients are significant at the 5 per cent level except when indicated with [a], which denotes insignificance at conventional levels.

The Grade Pay Structure

The differences between the average pay of the grades in the APS is shown in Table 3.6. The table reports the percentage difference between the average pay of the grade shown and the average pay of General Service Officer (GSO) grade. Again this has been constructed by taking the coefficients from Table 3.3 and converting them to percentage differences. The OLS regression that generated these coefficients included controls for the agency and state in which the employee works, their gender, education, age and length of service with the government.

Table 3.6 therefore reports only those differences in pay which are attributable to the grade in which the employee works. Thus employees in the most senior grades in the APS, the SES grade, on average earned 77.5 per cent more than the GSO grade in 1990, while those in the SO grade earned on average 32.7 per cent more, and those in the ASO grade earned 5.6 per cent more than the GSO grade. The Table reveals that over the six years to 1996 pay differentials between different grades widened substantially. By 1996 those in the SES grade were earning 105.5 per cent more than those in the GSO grade while those in the SO grade earned 53.6 per cent more and those in the ASO grade 11.0 per cent more.

This widening of the grade pay structure between 1990 and 1996 reflects moves to increase the competitiveness of the rates of pay offered to the most senior grades in the APS. The rates of pay of the most senior grades had by 1990 already fallen behind those available in similar jobs in the private section. Furthermore,

Table 1.4 revealed that between 1990 and 1995 there was a further widening of pay differentials in Australia. The most senior grades in the APS were therefore offered the largest pay settlements and some also benefited from the introduction of performance pay schemes. Appendix 3.1 which records the pay settlements for only the ASO and SO grades during the round of agency bargaining between 1993 and 1996 revealed that in many agencies those in the more senior grade, the SO grade, received higher pay awards than those in the ASO grade.

Table 3.6 The Grade Pay Structure in the APS
(Percentage Differences in Pay over GSO Grade)

	1990			1996		
	All Employees	Females	Males	All Employees	Females	Males
	(1)	(2)	(3)	(4)	(5)	(6)
SES	77.5	95.9	75.4	105.5	124.5	103.3
SO	32.7	44.5	31.7	53.6	67.8	52.1
ASO	5.6	11.1	6.1	11.0	18.3	11.2
OTHER	26.1	35.1	25.5	36.0	43.6	35.8

Notes: a. Constructed from the coefficients reported in Table 3.3 where the coefficients have been converted to percentage differences by: $(\exp(\beta)-1)*100$.

b. All coefficients are significant at the 5 per cent level.

Table 3.6 also reveals a much greater dispersion in women's pay than in men's pay in both 1990 and 1996. This is because of the differences in the grade distribution of men and women in the APS is the much greater dispersion in women's pay. Relatively few of the women working in the APS were employed on the SES and SO grades. Only 0.36 per cent of all women working in the APS in 1990 were employed in the SES grade and only 4.7 of women were in the SO grade in that year. In contrast 2.4 per cent of all men working in the APS were employed in the SES grade and 13.2 per cent were employed in the SO grade. Table 2.4 also revealed that over the period between 1990 and 1996 there had been an improvement in the representation of women in those two senior grades. In 1996, 0.75 per cent of all women in the APS were working in the SES grade and 8.7 were in the SO grade. However in both years most women were still to be found in the lowest paying grades in the APS, and the consequences of this are revealed in Table 3.6.

Accounting for the Changes in Pay Growth

One of the principal motivations for the introduction of decentralised pay setting is to allow departments and agencies to adjust the relative pay of different grades, to reform their pay structure. Devolved pay setting offers managers the opportunity to construct new pay structures which reward more highly the particular skills and attributes of their workforce they believe are most important. To what extent did this happen with the move to agency bargaining in Australia? In Chapter 2, equation 6 we detailed a method for decomposing any change in average pay into that part of the change which was due to changing the structure of pay and that part of the change that resulted from changes in the composition of the workforce. Here we employ that technique to analyse pay growth in the APS between 1990 and 1996. Using the data from the regressions reported in Table 3.3, we distinguish how much of the change in the average level of pay in the APS between 1990 and 1996 was the result of changes in the returns to the various characteristics of employees recorded in Table 3.3 and how much was due to changes in the composition, of the APS workforce. Table 3.7 reports the results of this exercise.

During the period 1990 to 1996, Australia retained a centrally determined job classification, or grading, structure while moving to agency bargaining. The maintenance of a common grading structure alongside agency bargaining meant that agencies were not able to change the grading system in an effort to control labour costs. They were not therefore free to change the composition of the agency workforce as they might have wished. Nonetheless, the occupational composition of the workforce in the different agencies which comprise the APS is still likely to have changed between 1990 and 1996 as the shares of employment in the different grades changed due to differences in recruitment and wastage rates between the grades over the period.

Table 3.7, row 1, shows that for the APS workforce taken as a whole, changes in the characteristics of the workforce in the APS accounted for the major part of the total growth in real pay over the period 1990 to 1996. Real pay grew by 19.0 between 1990 and 1996 and 55.4 per cent of this growth was due to the changing composition of the APS workforce, 10.5 of the 19 percentage point increase over the period was due to changes in the characteristics of the APS workforce. The remaining 44.6 per cent was due to changes in the APS pay structure. One aspect of the change in pay structure was detailed above, the move to pay employees in the higher grades in the APS more. Table 3.7 reveals that because these top groups account for a very small share of total employment, such changes in pay structure have only a small impact on the overall pay growth that occurred over the period. The picture is similar for men and women. 50.9 per cent of the growth in pay of men over the period 1990-1996 was accounted for by changes in the composition of the workforce, while 59.2 per cent of the pay growth of women was also accounted for by changes in the characteristics of the workforce. Thus changes in pay structure accounted for, less than half, 40.8 and 49.1 per cent for women and men respectively, of the growth in real pay over this period.

Table 3.7 Reimers Decomposition of Average Real Pay Growth in the APS

	All Employees		
	Changes in pay structure	Changes in characteristics	Total pay growth
	(1)	(2)	(3)
All Employees			
Overall	44.6	55.4	19.0
Personal characteristics	7.2	43.7	
Region	4.9	2.4	
Department	-6.0	-0.6	
Grade	38.6	9.8	
Females			
Overall	40.8	59.2	22.4
Personal characteristics	7.6	47.4	
Region	2.0	2.2	
Department	-2.9	-0.1	
Grade	34.1	9.7	
Males			
Overall	49.1	50.9	16.3
Personal characteristics	3.7	39.4	
Region	7.3	2.6	
Department	-9.1	-0.8	
Grade	47.2	9.7	

Notes: a. Total Pay Growth is the real average growth rate of pay from 1990 to 1996 in percentage terms.

b. The figures in the 'Overall' rows are the percentage contribution toward Total Pay Growth of changes in pay structure and changes in characteristics.

c. The figures in the other rows are the percentage contribution to the Overall differential by each of the four sets of variables controlled for in the regressions. The numbers contained in each column sum to the number in the 'Overall' row for that column. The sum across columns of all four rows will be 100.

Table 3.7 also reveals the relative contribution to pay growth of those characteristics of the APS workforce reported in Table 3.3. These characteristics have been placed in four groups. Those labelled Region (State), Department and Grade include all the variables listed below those heads in Table 3.3. The remaining variables, Gender, Tenure, Age and Educational Qualifications comprise the group, Personal Characteristics.

It is clear that by far the most significant change in the characteristics of the APS workforce between 1990 and 1996 which contributed to the pay growth over this period was the change in personal characteristics. Earlier it was revealed that the workforce had become older and more educated and both of these features are associated with higher pay. This element alone accounted for over three quarters of the change in the characteristics of the APS workforce. Changes in the grade structure of the APS were also an important feature of the changes in the characteristics of the APS workforce over the period. Table 3.7 reveals that changes in the APS pay structure accounted for almost half, 44.6 per cent of the pay growth of all employees between 1990 and 1996. It also reveals that by far the largest part, 38.6 out of the total 44.6 percentage points, was accounted for by changes in the relative rewards to different grades.

Thus, two factors appear to explain most of the pay growth that occurred in the APS between 1990 and 1996. First a change in the composition of the APS workforce towards a more highly educated workforce, and second, a change in the grade pay structure, with as we saw above, large pay increases being achieved by the most senior grades in the APS. Table 3.7 reveals that these two developments explain the major part of the pay growth of both men and women in the APS between 1990 and 1996.

Conclusion

There have been important changes in the pay structure of the APS during the six years between 1990 and 1996. The period witnessed substantial real pay growth; overall it ran at nearly 3 per cent per annum, so that by 1996, pay had grown by 19 per cent in real terms. However, there was substantial variation in the rate of pay growth between different grades, between difference departments and agencies while in general women did better than men.

The most senior grades, Senior Executives, and the lowest grade, General Service Officer experienced greater real pay growth than the middle grades in the APS. The result was that in the lower half of the pay distribution, pay inequality fell, while in the upper half of the pay distribution, pay inequality grew. Overall the impact of the narrowing of the distribution at the bottom offset the widening at the top so that the overall distribution showed no change over the period. However, within both the male and the female wage structure, when analysed separately, it was found that there was a modest widening of pay differentials over the period. Moreover, this was reflected in the grade pay structure. The period 1990 to 1996 revealed an increase in the relative pay of those in the more senior grades in the APS.

When we dug more deeply, we found that the causes of the growth in real pay were the substantial change in the characteristics of the APS workforce which by 1996 was a more highly educated workforce with a higher proportion of graduates than there had been in 1990. The second major explanation for pay growth over this period was the change in the pay structure detailed above with the largest increases targeted on the most senior grades.

What part had the move to agency bargaining played in these developments? Clearly the impact of agency bargaining was substantially reduced by the effects of the foldback arrangements which resulted in all agencies receiving very similar pay awards by the end of the period studied here. Yet though the average pay increases across all employees was very similar across the different agencies the freedom granted by agency bargaining was exploited by agencies. Agency bargaining permitted changes in the APS pay structure and allowed the largest pay increases to be awarded to the most senior grades. This freedom to differentiate between the pay increases awarded different groups of employees appears to be one of the more tangible achievements of agency bargaining.

References

Blau, F. and Kahn, L. (1996) 'International Differences in Male Wage Inequality: Institutions versus Market Forces', *Journal of Political Economy*, 104(4): 791-837.

Borland, J. (1996) 'Earnings Inequality in Australia: Changes and Causes', ANU mimeo.

Borland, J., Hirschberg, J. and Lye, J. (1998) 'Earnings of Public Sector and Private Sector Employees in Australia: Is There a Difference?', *Economic Record*, 74: 36-53.

Brown, W. and Fuller, D. (1978) 'The Impact of Over-Award Pay Upon the Australian Wage Structure', *Australian Bulletin of Labour*, 5: 34-42.

Deery, S. J. and Plowman, D. H, (1991) *Australian Industrial Relations* (3rd Ed), London, McGraw Hill.

Department of Industrial Relations (1995) *Industrial Manager*, Canberra.

Department of Industrial Relations (1995) *Industrial Manager Special Issue*, Canberra.

Department of Industrial Relations (1995) 'Adopting Continuous Improvement at the Department of Industry, Science and Technology,' *Towards a Better APS*, Profile #1, Canberra.

Department of Industrial Relations (1995) 'Pursuing Best Practices at Attorney-General's', *Towards a Better APS*, Profile #2, Canberra.

Department of Industrial Relations (1995) 'Implementing Workplace Reform at the Office of the Commonwealth Director of Public Prosecutions', *Towards a Better APS*, Profile #3, Canberra.

Department of Industrial Relations (1995) 'Using Performance Indicators for Success at the Australian Industrial Property Organizations', *Towards a Better APS*, Profile #4, Canberra.

Department of Industrial Relations (1995) 'Excelling in a Commercial Environment at the Australian Property Group', *Towards a Better APS*, Profile #5, Canberra.

Department of Industrial Relations (1996) *APS Agency Agreements and Innovation Employment Contract: A Resource Guide*, Canberra.

Kornfeld, R. (1993) 'The Effects of Union Membership on Wages and Employee Benefits: The Case of Australia', *Industrial and Labor Relations Review*, 47: 114-28.

Metcalf, D., Hansen, K. and Charlwood, A. (2000) 'Unions and the Sword of Justice: Unions and Pay Systems, Pay Inequality, Pay Discrimination and Low Pay', *Centre for Economic Performance*, Discussion Paper 452.

Niland, J., Brown, W. and Hughes, B. (1991) 'Breaking New Ground: Enterprise Bargaining and Agency Agreements for the Australian Public Service. A Report for the Australian Minister of Industrial Relations', Canberra.

Norris, K. (1996) *The Economics of Australian Labour Markets*, Melbourne, Longman.

O'Brien, J. (1995) 'Workplace Productivity Bargaining in the Australian Public Service' in J. Stewart (ed.) *From Hawke to Keating*, Centre for Research in Public Sector Management, Canberra, University of Canberra: 85-102.

Organization for Economic Co-operation and Development (1993) *Employment Outlook*, Paris, OECD.

Organization for Economic Co-operation and Development (1994) 'Collective Bargaining: Levels and Coverage', Chapter 5, *Employment Outlook*, Paris, OECD.

Plowman, D. (1986) 'Developments in Australian Wage Determination 1953-83: The Institutional Dimension', in J. Niland (ed.) *Wage Fixation - Australia*, Australian Studies in Industrial Relations, St. Leonards, Australia, Allen and Unwin: 15-48.

Public Sector Union (1993) 'Special Delegates Bulletin,' *Agency Bargaining*, Braddon, Australia.

Public Service and Merit Protection Commission (1996) 'Average Earnings in the Public and Private Sectors', *State of the Service Paper, No. 13*.

Reith, P. K. (1996) 'Towards a Best Practice Australian Public Service', Discussion Paper, Australian Government Printing Service, Canberra.

Smith, B. W. (1996) 'Average Earnings in the Public and Private Sectors', *Public Service and Merit Protection Commission: Working Papers in Statistics*, No. 1.

Vella, F. (1993) 'Gender Roles, Occupational Choice and Gender Wage Differential', *Economic Record*, 69 (207): 382-92.

Yates, B. (1998) 'Workplace Relations and Agreement Making in the Australian Public Service', *Australian Journal of Public Administration*.

Appendix 3.1   Timing and Size of Pay Increases under Agency Bargaining between 1993 and 1996

Australian Public Service-Administrative Service Officer (ASO) and Senior Officer Grade (SOG) A, B and C (Service-wide increases in bold)

Year	Month	Agency (coverage), date or chronological order and amount – same for all grades unless otherwise stated
1991	Aug	**ACCORD MARK VI AGREEMENT (Service-wide), 15th, 2.5%.** **Also lump sum (Service-wide) 16 May - 15 Aug, $12/week**
1992	Dec	**1992-94 APS AGREEMENT (Service-wide), 4th, 2%**
		Defence (ASO), 4%
1993	Mar	**1992-94 APS FRAMEWORK AGREEMENT (Service-wide), 1st, 1.4%**
1994	Jan	Australian Maritime Safety Authority (ASO, SOG), 2%
	Feb	Veteran's Affairs (ASO), 2%
	Mar	**1992-94 APS FRAMEWORK AGREEMENT (Service-wide), 1st, 1.5%**
		Australian Taxation Office (ASO, SOGA, SOGB, SOGC), 2%
	Apr	-
	May	Veteran's Affairs (SOG), 2%
	June	• Comcar (Car Driver), 1.4%
		• Comcar (TO, ASO), 1.4%
		• Australian Industrial Property Organisation (ASO, SOG), 1%
		• Employment, Education and Training (ASO, SOG), 2%
		• Australian Customs Service (ASO, SOG), 2%
	July	• Asset Services - DAS (ASO), 2%
		• Attorney-General's (ASO, SOG), 2%
		• Commonwealth Law Enforcement Board (ASO, SOG), 2%
		• DAS Removals - Dept of Administrative Services (ASO, SOG), 1.5%
		• Aboriginal and Torres Strait Islander Commission (ASO, SOG), 2%
		• Australian Property Group - Dept of Administrative Services (SOGA, SOGB, SOGC), $2000, $2000, $750 pa respectively
		• Australian Quarantine Inspection Service (ASO), 2%
		• DAS fleet (ASO, SOG), 2%
		• Immigration and Refugee Review Tribunal (ASO, SOGA, SOGB, SOGC) 2%, 2.4%, 2.4%, 2.4%
		• Immigration Review Tribunal (ASO, SOGA, SOGB, SOGC), 2%, 2.4%, 2.4%2.4%
		• Industry, Science & Technology; Industry, Research & Development Board; Textiles, Clothing and Footwear Development Authority (ASO, SOG), 2%, 2%[a]
		• Primary Industries and Energy (ASO), 2%
		• Social Security (ASO, SOG), 2%
		• Transport (ASO), 2%
		• Worksafe Australia (ASO, SOG), 2%

	Aug	•	Federal Court of Australia (ASO), 2%
		•	Human Services and Health (ASO), 2.5%
	Sept	•	Australian Industrial Property Organisation (ASO, SOG), 1%
		•	Australian Valuation Office-DAS(ASO), 1%
		•	Australian Securities Commission (ASO, SOGA, SOGB, SOGC), 4%, 5.5%, 5.5%, 4%
	Oct	•	AUSLIG-Dept of Administrative Services, (ASO, SOG), 2%
		•	Australian Property Group-Dept of Administrative Services (ASO, SOG), 3%,
		•	Comcar (Car Driver), 6th, 1.4% and one off $400
		•	Joint House Department (ASO, SOG), 2%,
	Nov	•	Foreign Affairs (ASO, SOG), 1.5%
		•	Transport (SOGA, SOGB, SOGC), 1%, 1%, 2%
	Dec	•	Aboriginal Hostels Limited (ASO, SOG), 2%
		•	Australian Maritime Safety Authority (ASO, SOG), 2%
		•	Australian Taxation Office (ASO1 to SOGC), 2%
		•	Australian Taxation Office (ASO1 to SOGC), 3%
		•	Industrial Relations, Affirmation Action Agency, Remuneration Tribunal, Defence Force
		•	Remuneration Tribunal (ASO, SOGA, SOGB, SOGC), 1%, 2%,2%, 1%
		•	Defence (ASO, SOG), 2%, 4%
		•	Spectrum Management Agency (ASO), 1%
		•	Veteran's Affairs (ASO, SOG), 2%
		•	Comcar Australia, $1000
		•	DAS Interiors (ASO), 2%
1995	Jan	•	Royal Australian Mint (ASO), 2%

PAY FOLDBACK (ASO, SOG), 12th, UP TO 2%

		•	DAS fleet (ASO, SOG), 2%
		•	Employment, Education and Training (ASO, SOG), 1.5%
	Feb	•	Aboriginal Hostels Limited (ASO), 2%
		•	Asset Services-DAS (ASO), 2%
		•	Australian Valuation Office-DAS (ASO), 2%
	Mar	•	Aboriginal and Torres Strait Islander Commission (ASO, SOG), 1%
		•	Australian Quarantine Inspection Service (ASO), 2%
		•	Primary Industries and Energy (ASO), 2%
	Apr	•	AUSLIG-Dept of Administrative Services, (ASO, SOG), 2%
		•	Australian Property Group-Dept of Administrative Services (ASO, SOG), 1%

PAY FOLDBACK (ASO, SOG), 6th, UP TO 2%[b]

		•	DAS Removals-Dept of Administrative Services (ASO, SOG), 1.5%
		•	Joint House Department (ASO, SOG), 2%
		•	Transport (ASO, SOGA, SOGB, SOGC), 1%, 4%, 4%, 1%
	May		DAS Interiors (ASO), 1%

June	**PAY FOLDBACK (SOGA, B, C), 29TH, UP TO 3.5%, 3.5%, 1.5%**[b,c]
July	• Industry, Science & Technology; Industry, Research & Development Board; Textiles, Clothing and Footwear Development Authority (ASO, SOG), 2%
	1995 - 1996 APS AGREEMENT (Service-wide), 13th, 2%
	• Attorney General's (ASO, SOG), 2%
	• Commonwealth Law Enforcement Board (ASO, SOG), 2%
	• Immigration and Refugee Review Tribunal (ASO, SOGA, SOGB, SOGC), 1%, 3.1%, 3.1%, 0.6%
	• Immigration Review Tribunal (SOGA, SOGB, SOGC), 3.1%, 3.1%, 0.6%
	• Industrial Relations, Affirmative Action Agency; Remuneration Tribunal; Defence Force
	• Remuneration Tribunal (ASO, SOGA, SOGB, SOGC), 1%, 3%, 3%, 2%
	• Social Security (ASO, SOG), 1%
	• Worksafe Australia (ASO, SOG), 1%
Aug	AUSLIG-Dept of Administrative Services, (ASO, SOG), 25% of net operating profit (lump sum)
Sept	• DAS Interiors (ASO), 1%
	• Foreign Affairs (ASO, SOG), 1.5%
	• Australian Industrial Property Organisation (ASO, SOG), up to 2%
Oct	Royal Australian Mint (ASO), 2%
Nov	-
Dec	Spectrum Management Agency (ASO), 12th, 1%
1996 Mar	**1995-1996 APS AGREEMENT (Service-wide), 7th, 1.6%**
Oct	**1995-1996 APS AGREEMENT (Service-wide), 17th, 2%**

Notes: a.   Also one off payments: SOGA - $2000; SOGB - $1900; SOGC - $650.

b.   Conditions for foldback increases were covered under the 1994–1995 Interim Agreement. The foldback increases were to allow employees from all agencies to achieve a minimum 4% increase in pay.

c.   The 29 June increase in SO pay was 'linked to the replacement of the performance pay system and addressed the discrepancies between agencies caused by the widespread pooling of performance pay allocations under agency bargaining' *Industrial Manager Special Issue,* November 1995, p7.

d.   For changes in other conditions of service and more detail on specific aspects of the reforms see the Department of Industrial Relations, 1995 and 1996 reports listed in the References

Appendix 3.2 Australian Civil Service Departments and Agencies

Variable Name	Description
ABARE	Australian Bureau of Agriculture and Research Economics
ABS	Australian Bureau of Statistics
ACCC	Australian Competition and Consumer Commission
ADMIN	Administrative Services
AEC	Australian Electoral Commission
AGPS	Aboriginal Government Publishing Service
AGSO	Australian Geological Survey Organisation
AIDAB	Australian International Development Assistance Bureau
AIPO	Australian Industrial Property Organisations
ANAO	Australian National Audit Office
ANCA	Australian Nature Conservation Agency
ARCHIVES	Australian Archives
ATO	Australian Taxation Office
ATSIC	Aboriginal and Torres Strait Islander Commission
ATTGEN	Attorney General
AWM	Australian War Memorial
COMCARE	Comcare
COMSUPER	Commonwealth Superannuation Commission
CUSTOMS	Australian Customs Service
DEETYA	Employment, Education, Training and Youth Affairs
DEFENCE	Defence
DFAT	Foreign Affairs and Trade
DIR	Department of Industrial Relations
DPIE	Primary Industry and Energy
DPP	Director of Public Prosecutions
DVA	Veterans' Affairs
FINANCE	Department of Finance
HEALTH	National Occupational Health and Safety Commission
IMMIG	Immigration and Multicultural Affairs
INDCOM	Industry Commission
ISC	Insurance and Superannuation Commission
NCA	National Crime Authority
NLA	National Library of Australia
PMC	Prime Minister and Cabinet
PSMPRA	Public Service and Merit Protection Review Agency
SOCSEC	Social Security
TREASURY	Treasury
WEATHER	Bureau of Meteorology

Chapter 4

Sweden

Introduction

It has frequently been claimed that after the Second World War, Sweden had one of the most highly centralised systems of wage bargaining in the world. The level of co-ordination between employees and employers in Swedish labour markets may well have been among the highest in the world during the first three decades after the war, but since the mid 1980s there have been substantial changes in the way that wages are determined. In particular there has been a move to local bargaining in both the private and public sectors. This move started in the private sector in the mid eighties but has also been pronounced in the Swedish central government sector. Though an element of local pay determination had been a feature of the central agreements covering central government employees throughout the 1980s, in 1989 the central grading system was abolished and a system of individual and differentiated pay was introduced.

This chapter analyses the changing nature of the bargaining which determines the pay and conditions of Swedish central government employees. It details the changes that have occurred in the bargaining framework, and the recent effects of these changes on the pay structure, and on the pay rates and dispersion of pay within the civil service. To set the context in which the changes have occurred, the first section details the recent history of public and private pay determination in Sweden and looks at previous research into changes in the public and private sector wage structures and relativities in Sweden. The following section outlines the motivation for reform in the determination of pay in the Swedish civil service and a further two sections analyse the effects of the decentralisation of pay on central government pay structure.

Private Sector Wage Determination

Historically, Sweden has had a highly disciplined and centralised system of pay determination. High rates of unionisation and membership of employers organisations facilitated a system in which a small number of central negotiations between unions and employers set the pay of the vast majority of the workforce. At the start of the 1990s, unions represented around 90 per cent of all employees and associations of business organisations covered 70 per cent of employees (Edin and Zetterberg, 1992). These institutions date back to 1889, when the Swedish

Confederation of Trade Unions (LO)[1] was formed, and to 1902, when the Swedish Employers' Confederation (SAF) was formed. The first important agreement between these two groups was in 1906 when the SAF recognised the right of workers to organise into trade unions and negotiate over pay and conditions and the LO recognised the right of employers to manage (Olsson, 1991). A second landmark agreement was made in 1938 when the Saltsjöbaden Agreement was concluded. This agreement formalised the rules for negotiation and conflict between employers and trade unions, and led to the formation of a labour market committee, made up of the LO, SAF and neutral representatives, who had the responsibility for interpreting and enforcing the agreement (Olsson, 1991). The Saltsjöbaden Agreement was based on two preconditions that were very similar to the 1906 agreement: first that the trade union movement would pursue a moderate pay policy and leave employers to manage companies and second that employers were to accept the power of trade unions. (Statstjänstemannaförbundet, 1997b). These institutional arrangements provided the foundations for centralised agreements but the main impetus toward centralised bargaining came later in the nineteen fifties. In 1952 at the urging of the SAF, the LO and the SAF signed the first of a series of centralised wage agreements.[2]

One element of the framework of labour law in Sweden which is frequently remarked upon is the Codetermination Act of 1977. This bill set down general conditions concerning industrial relations and identified the rights of the two sides of the bargaining process.[3] Rules were established across a wide range of different issues, the most important of which concerned: the right to establish trade unions; the right of these trade unions to negotiate over terms and conditions of employment and to establish collective agreements; the obligation for employers to inform the negotiating parties prior to decisions on important changes in a company's activities and to supply information on production and economic results; the obligation to maintain industrial peace, and the role of conciliation and the rules governing industrial disputes. The Act stipulated that, like other labour legislation, it was a 'skeleton law', which meant that its provisions were guidelines which could be superseded in collective agreements. When taken together with the system of centralised wage negotiation which had been established over twenty years before, this combination of centralised wage agreements and co-determination came to be characterised in the economics and industrial relations literature as 'The Swedish Model'.

In the late nineteen sixties and seventies, tensions emerged that began to destabilise the centralised system of wage determination. 'Wage drift' – locally determined increases in wages beyond those agreed in the central agreements – increased, making it difficult for the LO to maintain its policy of narrow wage

---

[1] In the early years, the LO comprised almost exclusively blue collar unions. The white collar union confederation (TCO) was not formed until some time later.

[2] See Edgren *et al.* (1973) for a detailed evaluation of wage policy in Sweden during the post-war period.

[3] See the Swedish Ministry of Finance, (1995: 28-29) for a concise statement of these.

differentials. These tensions were particularly pronounced among blue – collar workers. Calmfors and Forslund (1991) estimate that because of wage drift at this time, individual wages were up to 50 per cent higher than the bargained wage, also called the 'wage norm'. This 'secondary' bargaining was also associated with a series of wildcat strikes and lockouts which further undermined the position of the LO as the representative employee organisation. Perhaps more fundamentally as Olsson (1991: pp. 33-4) points out, the Swedish model depended upon a growing economy where the growth could be divided amongst profit, wages and the public sector. During the nineteen fifties and sixties there had been strong growth in the Swedish economy but the oil shocks of the seventies reduced the Swedish rate of growth while the early nineties witnessed a period of negative growth. These developments resulted in pressures to review the wage setting procedure.

These pressures emerged first in the nineteen eighties and were a function of both poorer rates of growth and the growing internationalisation of the largest Swedish firms. These firms were now more exposed to international competition and acutely aware of and concerned to contain domestic cost pressures. Ironically, it was the employers, who had first led Sweden into centralised wage setting, who now proposed to disengage. The move away from centralised bargaining began in the mid eighties when large firms in engineering and chemicals began to negotiate their own agreements and to include an element of contingent reward (profit related pay or profit sharing). In 1990 the SAF, led by the large employers, took the decision to disengage from further central bargaining over wages in the private sector (see Katz, 1993, and Robinson, 1995). Initially the central unions sought to retain centralised bargaining but those with a strong local structure began to recognise they might benefit and embraced decentralisation.

The Public and Private Sector Wage Structures

It is widely understood that the distribution of wages in Sweden is much narrower than that in many major industrialised nations. Edin and Zetterberg (1992) found a much narrower dispersion of wages in Sweden than in France, Germany, the UK and the USA. They also found far less inter-industry variation of wages in Sweden than in the US. The study, conducted using data from the early 1980s, revealed that most of the inter-industry variation in earnings in Sweden could be accounted for by differences in the human capital and demographic composition of the workforce. When controls for inter-industry differences in these characteristics and the work environment were introduced, the standard deviation of the inter-industry wage differentials dropped from 7.2 to 1.3 per cent. They further reported that the inter-industry dispersion of wages in the US was, for comparison, some ten times greater, than in Sweden even after the same controls were added. Variations in human capital appeared to account for relatively more of the inter-industry wage variation in Sweden than they did in the US, which suggested to the authors that it was the centralised system of wage determination that existed in Sweden at this time that accounted for the much narrower wage dispersion in that country.

A second study (Green *et al*, 1992) of Sweden and four other countries employed several different measures of inequality (variance of natural logarithm, Gini index, Theil index and the Atkinson measure) and also found that the dispersion of male earnings among these five countries was greatest in the US and least in Sweden. This study also revealed that there had been an increase in dispersion of male earnings in Sweden during the eighties which as we shall see later might be ascribed to a loosening of the centralised arrangements over this period.

During the sixties and seventies it was widely understood that wages in the tradable, manufacturing sector of the economy were determined first and were then followed by wages in the non-tradable sectors which attempted to imitate the pattern set by the earlier bargain. However, as public sector employment grew from 25 per cent of the labour force in 1965 to 41 per cent in 1990, it became less clear that private sector wages would continue to lead.

The linkages between wages in the public and private sectors in Sweden were examined in two articles by Holmlund and Ohlsson (1992) and Jacobson and Ohlsson (1994). Both studies found that the private sector 'Granger causes' both central and local government wages, although Holmlund and Ohlsson (1992) found some feedback effects as well. The same authors also reported a 20 per cent average wage premium in the public sector in the mid sixties which had been entirely eroded by 1976. They found that although the relative wages of public sector employees in central and local government improved again in the mid eighties, they fell once more in the last half of that decade. The study also reported that local government wages were greater than central government wages until the mid eighties, after which time they moved in parallel.

The only microeconomic study which has set out directly to analyse the wages of public and private sector employees in Sweden was by Andersson and Schager (1999). They found that in 1993 private sector employees received an hourly pay premium of approximately 5.8 per cent.[4] Using standard relative wage decomposition techniques, they found that only 2 percentage points of the premium was accounted for by the different productive characteristics of the public sector, leaving 3.8 percentage points of that premium due to the differences in wage structure. There was no analysis of movements in the earnings differential over time, however, so the effects of the reforms in central government pay bargaining could not be isolated.

---

[4] This study took a much broader definition of the public sector than Holmlund and Ohlsson (1992). They included all levels of government – central, county and local – plus state owned corporations.

Developments in Government Pay Determination

Pay in the public sector was not always determined through negotiation. According to Andersson and Schager (1999), before 1965 the government, after some consultation with trade union representatives, set wages unilaterally. However, in that year public sector trade unions were given the legal right to negotiate on behalf of central government workers. The employers side formed an employers organisation, called the National Collective Bargaining Office (see Swedish Ministry of Finance, 1995) to negotiate on behalf of the government. Later, this Office became the National Agency for Government Employers, the Arbetsgivarverket, or AgV, and on 1 July, 1994 the government delegated all central negotiating authority to the AgV. In 1996, the AgV covered 270 different agencies and was entirely financed by membership fees collected from these agencies (Andersson and Schager, 1999). The AgV negotiated with three main trade unions, the Swedish Confederation of Professional Associations, or SACO-S, which organised professional groups with university training, the Central Organisation of Salaried Employees, or TCO-F, which consisted of white collar workers in general and the police and military in particular; and the public sector of the Swedish Trade Union Confederation, SKRO, which organised blue-collar workers.

Until the early eighties, pay within central government was characterised by a very rigid pay and grading structure. In addition wage agreements were very centralised, and any negotiated increases applied to the entire civil service. Andersson and Schager (1999) suggest that this was a consequence of the policy of successive Social Democratic Governments which wanted to promote earnings equality. However, because this was not a policy pursued by the private sector, a gap soon emerged between the wages of many public and private sector employees. This gap has been referred to as the 'double imbalance' (see for example Zetterberg, 1988 and Schager, 1993) for it consisted of overpaying low skilled public sector workers and underpaying high skilled public sector workers relative to the private sector. This imbalance caused large tensions between the two sectors, because it resulted in a plentiful supply of low skilled labour to the public sector but made it difficult for the public sector to recruit and retain highly skilled workers.

In 1978 an element of decentralised bargaining over pay was introduced into the public sector. In that year, up to 1 per cent of pay was bargained over at the local level. A further break from the traditional centralised bargaining came in 1985 with the passage of a bill called Personnel Policy in the Government Sector. This bill formalised the process of decentralisation that had been started in 1978 and represented a substantial move away from the policy of equality of pay. The bill stated that pay policy in the different agencies should be set to allow for the efficient operation of and supply of services produced by the agency. Common grading across the civil service still survived, however, until the framework agreement of 1989 abolished the traditional grading system.[5]

Since 1989, pay negotiations have taken place on two levels. First, there is a central framework agreement negotiated between the AgV and the central government unions. This central agreement often, but not always, results in a minimum increase in pay and more importantly, also determines the scope for local pay increases. The central agreement establishes a 'pay kitty', and by negotiating a formula which determines each individual employees' contribution to the kitty, it also establishes the size of the kitty. The distribution of the kitty is then the subject of bargaining at a second level, at the local level, between the unions and individual agencies.

The amount of money available to the agencies for pay and other items of current expenditure is determined by the Ministry of Finance. The amount of money available to each agency, their cash limit or 'frame grant', is determined by a formula, which among other things, takes into account private sector wage movements. This 'frame grant' is determined through the budgetary process by the Ministry of Finance who inform the AgV, agencies and unions of the size of the grant and what assumptions they made about pay. However, the formula establishing the budget for the agency is only the starting point, for depending upon the political and economic climate, the central government may adjust the amount of funds this provides. If 'extra investment' is needed the amount provided will be adjusted up by the government, or if costs need to be controlled it will be adjusted down. No part of the frame grant is specifically identified for or set aside for pay increases.

The direct influence of the central government ends when the agencies funds have been set. Subsequently the AgV and the unions negotiate the central framework agreement by bargaining over the size of the pay kitty and the parameters that are to be established for local bargaining. The framework agreement determines the size of the pay kitty, and because it has, in effect, determined the average size of pay increase, it reflects the parties decision on the trade-off between wage increases and changes in employment. Once the framework agreement has been struck, the unions and separate agencies then bargain at the local level over the distribution of the agreed wage increases to determine how the increase will be distributed.

An example of this process is provided by Andersson and Schager (1999), who report the round of pay negotiations covering the 33 month period starting in July 1995. At the outset these negotiations provided for a minimum increase for all full-time central government employees of 1.8 per cent or 300SKr per month, whichever was the greater, from 1 July, 1995. However this was an interim payment for agreement was not reached until December 1995. The agreement that

---

[5] In 1991 the five level TNS system was introduced to provide a common method for classifying jobs in the public sector. Based on the BNT system then in operation in the private sector, it was also hoped that this would facilitate a comparison between jobs in the two sectors.

was eventually reached specified a total contribution per employee to the pay kitty of 9.7 per cent over the period 1 July, 1995 to 31 March, 1998. Distribution of the kitty occurred in three stages. The first interim payment was made on 1 July 1995 while the second was made on 1 January, 1996 and the final one on 1 January, 1997. At the second stage where a 4 per cent increase was made available for distribution in local negotiations, no minimum increase was guaranteed, except where there was failure to reach agreement in local negotiations in which case all employees in the relevant agency would receive 275SKr per month. At the final stage the amount available for distribution in local negotiations was on average 3.3 per cent subject to a minimum individual increase of 300SKr per month. However, at this last stage the minimum could be disregarded if an alternative distribution was agreed in local negotiations. Thus it can be seen that the system involves first a set of central negotiations which determine the size of the pay kitty, often articulated as the average size of contribution or the 'notional' wage increase, while, a second set of negotiations at the local level determine the precise distribution of the kitty.

Non-wage aspects of employment are negotiated at both the central and local level. Such things as pension schemes and severance pay provisions are centrally negotiated between the AgV and the Trade Unions. Other general conditions have gradually become the prerogative of local negotiations. Thus such things as compensation for travelling costs and allocation of working time have been delegated to local bargaining over the last several years. However, in principle, all pay and working conditions can be bargained over at the local level, and these agreements have precedence over any centrally negotiated contracts.

An essential feature of the Swedish system has been the move away from national pay scales to 'individual and differentiated pay'. Although in the first few years following their appointment all central government employees are paid under an incremental scale, they are soon on salaries where they have no entitlement to further increments. They can however, seek adjustment to their salaries in recognition of changes in responsibility, experience and performance, although these are by no means automatic. There are however exceptions, the police, armed services and judges continue to be paid under incremental scales.

Like the majority of public sector, central government has also moved away from a common grading structure. The TNS system enables them to slot jobs into a common classification system, so that when a job falls vacant the qualifications and experience appropriate to fill the vacancy can be easily identified. However the salary will be set at the level the agency regards as appropriate for the requirements of the job.

Yet even though every individual's salary is negotiated at the local level, this does not result in substantial differentiation between individuals doing similar jobs. This is because every individuals salary is open to public scrutiny and the effect of this openness, when combined with a history in which the emphasis has been on wage equality, is effectively to minimise differences between the pay of individuals doing the same job. Furthermore, there was no systematic evaluation of employee performance in the mid 1990s, pay related only indirectly to an individual's performance which further diminished the differences that might otherwise have existed within occupations. In consequence the pay increases negotiated in local bargaining tended to be awarded to groups of staff rather than to individuals. The principal cause of differentiation within occupations was the differential rates paid to new starters. However, this element would not be expected to have had any substantial impact on the overall wage structure analysed below because in 1993 and 1996 the proportion of the workforce hired since 1989 would still represent a small minority.

Motivation for Reform

Several reasons can be advanced to explain why Sweden chose such a radical path of reform. By the late 1980s the pressures to 'do something' were extreme. The labour market pressures resulting from the double imbalance meant that ways had to be found to pay more for scarce and higher level skills. The problem had been exacerbated by decentralised bargaining in the private sector which resulted in changes in the wage structure in that sector. The macroeconomic pressures to contain public expenditure were also considerable at this time. Public sector employment as a share of total employment grew sharply during the eighties and peaked in 1990. In addition, in each of the three years after 1990, the rate of growth of GNP was negative. The resulting pressures to contain public expenditure were by now immense and any adjustments to the central government wage structure had therefore to be achieved within a climate of financial restraint.

Sweden chose this particular path of reform for a variety of reasons. First the small scale of public sector commercial activities offered limited scope for privatisation; this would anyway not offer solutions to the problems in central government administration and local government. Second, administrative decentralisation has long been a feature of Swedish central government – separate agencies responsible for administering policy reported to each of the main Swedish governed ministries. Third, the strong public service ethic offered less scope for market testing for there was no real prospect that public services would be taken out of the hands of existing service providers. Most importantly the long established structure of agencies presented the foundations on which an alternative system of pay determination could be built. Swedish unions had a long history of negotiating over conditions of service other than pay at the agency level and thus had the organisational structure necessary to facilitate such a change. Once a system of cash limits had been established, trade unions saw agency bargaining as the best mechanism for exploiting the flexibilities that these new budgetary arrangements would entail.

Analysis of Civil Service Pay

Chapter 2 gave details of the civil service data used for Sweden. It reported that only those central government employees performing the same functions as the civil service in the other two countries were selected from the records of central government employees in Sweden for inclusion in this analysis. The dataset used in the analysis in this chapter includes part-time employees but earnings have been adjusted on to a full-time basis by adjusting by the number of hours worked. In this analysis the TNS sample is used for this enables us to distinguish the main occupational groups, the main grades, in the civil service. Details of the TNS dataset and the variables included in this analysis were reported in Tables 2.1 and 2.2.

Pay Growth and Dispersion by Grade and Department

Table 4.1 reports changes in real median pay from 1993 and 1996 by grade and department for both males and females. Overall, there was an increase in real median pay of 5.7 per cent for this sample. The rate of growth was somewhat faster for females (6.2 per cent) compared to males (5.0 per cent), although the differences are much smaller than what we observed for Australia. Table 4.1 also reveals substantial variation between departments in the median level of pay and in the change in median pay. Although Labour had the highest median pay for women in 1990 (SKr14,780) and Trade had the highest median pay for men in 1990 (SKr20,171), Environment by 1996 was, by a clear margin, the department with the highest median rate of pay at SKr22,469 per month for men and SKr17,084 for women. Justice was the department with the lowest rate of pay for males (SKr14,749) and females (SKr13,479) in 1996. There was also a clear and substantial difference between the average levels of pay in each of the five grades. Pay rose substantially with movements up the hierarchy: the pay of the highest ranking civil servants was 2.26 times as great as that of the lowest, Assistants in 1993, growing to 2.35 times in 1996.

Over the three years from 1993 to 1996 there was quite a wide variation in the rate of increase of average pay between departments. For both men and women, real median pay increased fastest in Environment and least in Trade. A notable feature of this period was that, with few exceptions, median pay increased faster for women than for men. Among the Highest Ranking Civil Servants the pay of females increased by 10.1 per cent while that of males increased by only 7.6 per cent. There were very substantial changes in the occupational composition of these groups during this period which helps account for the differences in the growth of average pay for men and women.

Table 4.1 Real Median Monthly Pay by Grade and Department in the Swedish Civil Service in 1993 and 1996

(In 1993 prices, SKr)	All Employees			Females			Males		
	1993	1996	% Change	1993	1996	% Change	1993	1996	% Change
	(1)	(2)	(3)	(4)	(5)	(6)	(7)	(8)	(9)
All Employees	14,314	15,137	5.7	13,187	14,001	6.2	15,994	16,796	5.0
GRADES									
Highest Ranking Civil Servants	27,945	29,968	7.2	26,423	29,083	10.1	28,141	30,270	7.6
Qualified Administrators	21,311	22,559	5.9	20,313	21,610	6.3	21,655	22,832	5.4
Administrators	16,647	17,256	3.7	15,979	16,662	4.3	17,018	17,728	4.2
Qualified Assistants	13,767	14,156	2.8	13,346	13,724	2.8	14,400	14,822	2.9
Assistants	12,333	12,758	3.4	12,259	12,618	2.9	12,506	13,292	6.3
DEPARTMENTS									
Justice	12,978	13,547	4.4	12,978	13,479	3.9	13,863	14,749	6.4
Foreign Affairs	15,646	16,057	2.6	14,371	14,837	3.2	19,732	19,475	-1.3
Defence	14,706	15,304	4.1	12,926	13,547	4.8	15,662	15,865	1.3
Social Affairs	15,367	17,050	11.0	14,560	15,834	8.8	17,396	18,938	8.9
Transport	14,618	16,696	14.2	12,823	14,690	14.6	16,967	18,378	8.3
Finance	13,961	14,837	6.3	12,913	13,738	6.4	16,188	17,221	6.4
Education	14,560	15,016	3.1	14,314	14,837	3.7	15,522	15,536	0.1
Agriculture	14,059	15,092	7.3	13,253	14,341	8.2	14,603	16,414	12.4
Labour	15,851	16,796	6.0	14,780	15,228	3.0	16,498	17,996	9.1
Culture	13,749	15,320	11.1	13,602	15,031	10.5	14,214	15,945	12.2
Trade	15,321	15,520	1.3	13,643	14,270	4.6	20,171	18,880	-6.4
Public Affairs	13,849	15,122	9.2	12,823	13,820	7.8	17,292	17,662	1.9
Environment	14,415	19,573	35.8	13,368	17,084	27.6	16,899	22,469	33.0

Table 4.2 Pay Dispersion by Grade and Department in the Swedish Civil Service in 1993 and 1996

	All Employees						Females						Males					
	Standard Deviation		10/50 Ratio		90/50 Ratio		Standard Deviation		10/50 Ratio		90/50 Ratio		Standard Deviation		10/50 Ratio		90/50 Ratio	
	1993	1996	1993	1996	1993	1996	1993	1996	1993	1996	1993	1996	1993	1996	1993	1996	1993	1996
	(1)	(2)	(3)	(4)	(5)	(6)	(7)	(8)	(9)	(10)	(11)	(12)	(13)	(14)	(15)	(16)	(17)	(18)
All Employees	0.252	0.291	0.825	0.820	1.517	1.550	0.191	0.252	0.881	0.868	1.362	1.422	0.271	0.303	0.768	0.779	1.525	1.542
GRADES																		
Highest Ranking CS	0.218	0.225	0.774	0.787	1.323	1.315	0.219	0.211	0.791	0.785	1.320	1.276	0.216	0.228	0.782	0.787	1.322	1.318
Qualified Administrators	0.232	0.247	0.794	0.794	1.264	1.270	0.193	0.244	0.804	0.800	1.241	1.246	0.243	0.246	0.908	0.800	1.087	1.280
Administrators	0.148	0.168	0.860	0.842	1.225	1.269	0.131	0.149	0.876	0.856	1.206	1.235	0.152	0.177	0.864	0.837	1.235	1.281
Qualified Assistants	0.118	0.169	0.883	0.893	1.169	1.179	0.095	0.126	0.908	0.912	1.133	1.142	0.130	0.204	0.853	0.876	1.181	1.202
Assistants	0.095	0.225	0.917	0.907	1.121	1.134	0.084	0.222	0.922	0.915	1.102	1.106	0.116	0.226	0.908	0.879	1.161	1.172
DEPARTMENTS																		
Justice	0.198	0.274	0.925	0.904	1.274	1.349	0.140	0.193	0.928	0.909	1.151	1.177	0.351	0.507	0.850	0.816	2.028	2.102
Foreign Affairs	0.274	0.278	0.787	0.796	1.621	1.606	0.200	0.216	0.821	0.850	1.349	1.448	0.282	0.308	0.698	0.676	1.416	1.525
Defence	0.247	0.247	0.811	0.824	1.464	1.487	0.148	0.185	0.899	0.897	1.234	1.302	0.253	0.247	0.785	0.821	1.468	1.499
Social Affairs	0.302	0.482	0.813	0.762	1.667	1.662	0.241	0.327	0.847	0.820	1.498	1.559	0.351	0.638	0.734	0.689	1.848	1.777
Transport	0.285	0.383	0.790	0.766	1.632	1.581	0.204	0.305	0.886	0.850	1.394	1.461	0.295	0.409	0.709	0.721	1.511	1.490
Finance	0.251	0.260	0.831	0.815	1.533	1.540	0.198	0.214	0.883	0.865	1.401	1.429	0.272	0.275	0.763	0.769	1.533	1.508
Education	0.249	0.324	0.792	0.822	1.507	1.548	0.223	0.299	0.846	0.832	1.412	1.430	0.296	0.373	0.776	0.795	1.629	1.650
Agriculture	0.264	0.338	0.839	0.833	1.513	1.605	0.202	0.270	0.893	0.871	1.406	1.505	0.288	0.378	0.803	0.796	1.528	1.616
Labour	0.208	0.369	0.795	0.770	1.323	1.377	0.188	0.312	0.839	0.825	1.288	1.369	0.205	0.411	0.849	0.781	1.347	1.369
Culture	0.218	0.321	0.838	0.787	1.432	1.478	0.189	0.350	0.847	0.789	1.326	1.369	0.248	0.275	0.816	0.772	1.536	1.536

Table 4.2 (Cont.)

	All Employees						Females						Males					
	Standard Deviation		10/50 Ratio		90/50 Ratio		Standard Deviation		10/50 Ratio		90/50 Ratio		Standard Deviation		10/50 Ratio		90/50 Ratio	
	1993	1996	1993	1996	1993	1996	1993	1996	1993	1996	1993	1996	1993	1996	1993	1996	1993	1996
	(1)	(2)	(3)	(4)	(5)	(6)	(7)	(8)	(9)	(10)	(11)	(12)	(13)	(14)	(15)	(16)	(17)	(18)
Trade	0.310	0.390	0.751	0.812	1.639	1.579	0.251	0.489	0.829	0.846	1.523	1.508	0.293	0.278	0.656	0.813	1.355	1.533
Public Affairs	0.248	0.250	0.855	0.840	1.513	1.536	0.171	0.195	0.915	0.903	1.349	1.369	0.261	0.258	0.725	0.774	1.471	1.474
Environment	0.257	0.273	0.856	0.711	1.631	1.459	0.186	0.245	0.865	0.780	1.363	1.438	0.275	0.242	0.763	0.744	1.559	1.363

In almost all departments there was an increase in the dispersion of pay between 1993 and 1996. The dispersion of pay among males in the department shown in Table 4.2 as measured by the standard deviation ranges from 0.205 to 0.351 in 1993 (see column 13) and from 0.242 to 0.638 in 1996 (column 14), while among women it ranges from 0.148 to 0.251 in 1993 (column 7) and from 0.185 to 0.489 in 1996 (column 8). Evidently the dispersion of women's pay in each department is less than that of men but like men, dispersion has increased in almost every department over the period. Dispersion has also increased in every one of the grades with the single exception of the females in the Highest Ranking Civil Service grade. Again in each grade the dispersion of pay is less among women than it is among males. Evidently there was a fairly general increase in the dispersion of pay in the Swedish Civil Service over this relatively short period.

Regression Results

The results of the regressions are reported in Table 4.3. The OLS results reported here distinguish the effects on an employees pay of their gender, age, length of time in government service and length of time employed in the department in which they currently work, as well as the effects if the department, their grade and the region in which they work. The table shows that males earned 5.2 per cent more than females (0.051 log points) in 1993 but that the amount decreased to 4.6 per cent (0.045 log points) by 1996. As with Australia so in Sweden pay rose with age. In 1993 the age of maximum pay was essentially the same for both genders at 49.7 years but this had decreased slightly to 49.0 and 48.4 years for men and women respectively, by 1996.[6] The diminishing nature of the returns to age is indicated by the negative coefficient on age squared. Because this increased between 1993 and 1996 (become more negative), the age of maximum pay fell as indicated.

Pay is also shown to rise with years spent in government service. Each year of government service results in a small, but again diminishing, addition to pay and by 1996 this affect had vanished for males. In 1993 the annual increment to pay for males after 10 years service was 0.4 per cent, but by 1996 it was no longer significant. In 1993 women gained an additional 0.4 per cent from a further year of service after 10 years service but it had declined to 0.2 per cent in 1996. It is interesting to note that while years of government service enhance pay, years of service within a specific department or agency (TENAG) detract from pay. This is a similar result to that found in the earlier analysis of Anderson and Schager (1999). It would appear that the way to enhance pay is to move between departments, not stay in the same department. This might be interpreted as the reward for moving to more demanding, challenging work.

---

[6] See Chapter 3, equations (1) and (2), for the formulae for determining the age and tenure of maximum pay.

Table 4.3 Regression Results for 1993 and 1996 – Sweden

Variable	1993			1996		
	All Employees	Males	Females	All Employees	Males	Females
Male	(1)	(2)	(3)	(4)	(5)	(6)
	0.051	-	-	0.045	-	-
Age	0.019	0.024	0.016	0.029	0.032	0.024
Agesq	-1.91E-4	-2.30E-4	-1.56E-4	-2.96E-4	-3.25E-4	-2.48E-4
Tengov	5.74E-3	5.82E-3	4.05E-3	2.02E-3	5.68E-4[a]	2.66E-3
Tengovsq	-8.00E-5	-8.21E-5	-5.46E-5	-2.52E-5	5.66E-6[a]	-4.60E-5
Tenag	-6.98E-3	-0.011	-1.91E-3	-2.51E-3	-2.65E-3	-2.34E-3
Tenagsq	1.76E-4	3.07E-4	2.68E-5	4.57E-5	5.10E-5	4.52E-5
Full	0.017	0.033	0.015	0.070	0.173	0.048
REGION						
South	-0.062	-0.078	-0.051	-0.076	-0.092	-0.061
Central	-0.052	-0.063	-0.047	-0.077	-0.093	-0.064
North	-0.057	-0.071	-0.045	-0.066	-0.074	-0.058
DEPARTMENT/AGENCY						
Foreign Affairs	-7.33E-3	-0.046	2.37E-3[a]	0.029	0.030	0.029
Defence	0.054	0.020	0.044	0.085	0.090	0.059
Socialaf	0.053	0.022	0.057	0.025	-0.026	0.067
Transprt	0.013	-0.020	0.015	0.012	4.83E-3[a]	0.028
Finance	0.039	0.012	0.037	0.041	0.046	0.036
Educ	0.035	-0.040	0.058	0.039	0.019	0.047
Agri	-0.038	-0.109	0.028	0.011	-6.08E-4[a]	0.039
Labour	0.024	-0.030	0.049	0.018	-9.48E-3[a]	0.039
Culture	-0.013	-0.087	0.017	-0.036	-0.049	-0.023
Trade	0.024	6.61E-3	0.013	-1.48E-3[a]	-3.20E-3[a]	1.57E-5[a]
Pubaff	0.013	-0.029	0.018	7.86E-3	1.89E-3[a]	0.012
Environ	0.034	0.011[a]	0.028	1.78E-3[a]	-0.026	0.018
GRADE						
Highcs	0.860	0.864	0.867	0.922	0.930	0.903
Deptman	0.705	0.711	0.690	0.769	0.771	0.774
Qualad	0.463	0.467	0.466	0.516	0.526	0.504
Admin	0.268	0.279	0.263	0.297	0.303	0.293
Qualasst	0.098	0.121	0.087	0.106	0.115	0.100
Constant	8.948	8.920	9.016	8.795	8.664	8.915
Adjusted R2	0.75	0.708	0.738	0.618	0.61	0.557

Notes: a.   The omitted variables are the STOCKHOLM for region, the JUSTICE
            department and ASSISTANT for grade.
       b.   All coefficients are significant at the 5 per cent level except when indicated
            with [a], which denotes insignificance at conventional levels.

The Regional Pay Structure

Table 4.3 also reports the regional structure of pay in the Swedish civil service.
The coefficients from Table 4.3 have been transformed into percentage differences
in average pay from the omitted region, Stockholm and are reported in Table 4.4.
The Table shows that those working in Stockholm are the highest paid for those
working in the other three areas, the South, Central and Northern areas of the
country, were paid less than Stockholm in both 1993 and 1996. The Table also
shows that the difference in pay between those working in Stockholm and the other
three regions increased between 1993 and 1996. One of the opportunities afforded
by a decentralised pay system is to bring rates of pay into line with those in the
local market. Although the analysis for Sweden is conducted over a very short-time
period and we should not expect to observe big changes in just three years, it is
interesting to note the rise in the Stockholm pay premium which may be moving
slowly into line with that in the private sector in Stockholm. It is also interesting to
note that the Stockholm premium is less for women than for men. The Stockholm
premium was around 7 per cent for men in 1993 and 5 per cent for women in that
year, but rose to 9 per cent for men and nearly 7 per cent for women in 1996.

**Table 4.4 The Regional Structure of Pay in the Swedish Civil Service
(Percentage differences from pay in Stockholm)**

	1993			1996		
	All Employees	Females	Males	All Employees	Females	Males
	(1)	(2)	(3)	(4)	(5)	(6)
South	-6.0	-5.0	-7.5	-7.3	-5.9	-8.8
Central	-5.1	-4.6	-6.1	-7.4	-6.2	-8.9
North	-5.5	-4.4	-6.9	-6.4	-5.6	-7.1

Notes: a.   Constructed from the coefficients in Table 4.3 where the coefficients are
            converted to percentage differences by: $(\exp(\beta)-1)*100$
       b.   All coefficients are significant at the 5 per cent level.

The Departmental Pay Structure

Table 4.3 also reports the inter-departmental pay structure where the analysis
focuses on the thirteen largest departments in the Swedish Civil Service. The
coefficients from the OLS regression have been used to calculate the percentage

differences between the average pay of all employees in twelve of these departments and the average pay in a reference department which is the Justice Department. The OLS allows us to report these percentage differences after controlling for all the other independent influences on pay captured in the regression. These percentage differences are recorded in Table 4.5.

The importance of controlling for other influences on pay by the use of multiple regression techniques is well illustrated. Table 4.1 reported that the Environment department was the highest paying for all employees in 1996 by some margin. But once we control for the grade and regional structure of employment and for characteristics of the workforce, this is no longer the case. Defence emerges as the highest paying department in 1996. Table 4.5 reveals a very narrow inter-department pay structure in 1993 with the range between average pay in the highest paying department, Defence, and the lowest, Agriculture, less than 10 percentage points. Even though the inter-department pay structure has become more dispersed by 1996 it is still very narrow. In that year, Defence was still the highest paying but now Culture was the lowest paying and the range between the highest and lowest had grown slightly to 12.4 percentage points.

The summary statistic, maximum minus minimum percentage difference reports the difference between the highest and lowest paying departments and it therefore constitutes one measure of the degree of dispersion of the inter-departmental pay structure. An alternative measure is the standard deviation of the percentage differences in average pay from the reference department. Table 4.5 shows that this also increased between 1993 and 1996. Thus the inter-departmental pay structure has become a little more dispersed as a result of the move to agency bargaining in the Swedish Civil Service.

We noted above that a study of the public and private sectors in Sweden in the 1980s (Edin and Zetterberg, 1992) concluded that the inter-industry dispersion of earnings was much narrower in Sweden than in either of the other major European countries or the US. This study included a wider set of control variables than are available here. Most importantly they were able to control for employees education. They found that after controlling for differences in the human capital and demographic composition of the workforce and the working environment the standard deviation of the inter-industry wage differentials was just 1.3 per cent. They concluded that the centralised system of wage determination that existed in Sweden at that time accounted for the much narrower inter-industry wage dispersion in Sweden. It is therefore interesting to note that even though educational controls are missing from the analysis in this chapter, the inter-departmental structure is still found to be very narrow. But there also suggestions that as the grip of the central agreements relaxed, with the move to agency bargaining, the inter-departmental pay structure has become more dispersed.

Table 4.5 The Departmental Pay Structure in Sweden
(Percentage Differences in Pay from the Justice Department)

	1993			1996		
	All Employees	Females	Males	All Employees	Females	Males
	(1)	(2)	(3)	(4)	(5)	(6)
SUMMARY STATISTICS						
Maximum - minimum percentage difference	9.3	12.6	6.0	12.4	14.2	9.2
Standard deviation of percentage difference	2.8	4.1	1.9	3.0	3.8	2.6
DEPARTMENTAL DIFFERENCES						
FOREIGN AFFAIRS	-0.7	-4.5	0.2	2.9	3.0	2.9
DEFENCE	5.5	2.0	4.5	8.9	9.4	6.1
SOCIALAF	5.4	2.2	5.9	2.5	-2.6	6.9
TRANSPORT	1.3	-2.0	1.5	1.2	0.5	2.8
FINANCE	4.0	1.2	3.8	4.2	4.7	3.7
EDUCATION	3.6	-3.9	6.0	4.0	1.9	4.8
AGRI	-3.7	-10.3	2.8	1.1	-0.1	4.0
LABOUR	2.4	-3.0	5.0	1.8	-0.9	4.0
CULTURE	-1.3	-8.3	1.7	-3.5	-4.8	-2.3
TRADE	2.4	0.7	1.3	-0.1	-0.3	0.0
PUBAFF	1.3	-2.9	1.8	0.8	0.2	1.2
ENVIRON	3.5	1.1	2.8	0.2	-2.6	1.8

Notes: a. Constructed from the coefficients in Table 4.3 where the coefficients are converted to percentage differences by: $(exp(\beta)-1)*100$.
  b. All coefficients are significant at the 5 per cent level.

The Grade Pay Structure

Table 4.6 reports the grade pay structure, where the percentage differences in pay between the grades shown and the reference grade, which is the Assistant Grade, have been calculated using the coefficients in Table 4.3. Here we also split the most senior grade, comparable to the Senior Service in Australia and Senior Civil Servants in the UK, into two categories. HIGHCS represents the most senior civil servants in Sweden, who comprised less than 1 per cent of all civil servants in Sweden in 1995 and 1996 and DEPTMAN, Department and Agency Managers who comprised less than 3 per cent of all Swedish Civil Servants in these same years (see Table 2.6).

Table 4.6 reveals a number if interesting features. First, the grade pay structure was almost identical for men and women in 1993. Males in the very highest grades, HIGHCS, were paid 138.0 per cent more on average than the Assistant grade while women in the same grade were paid 137.3 per cent more than assistants. Further down the grade hierarchy the percentage differences between the pay of men and women in each grade and those of the same gender in the Assistant Grade were in all cases almost identical. Second, there was a widening of pay differentials between 1993 and 1996. Moreover, this widening occurred across the complete grade hierarchy and occurred to a very similar degree among both men and women.

Within the three-year interval between 1993 and 1996 the pay differentials between the highest paid civil servants, HIGHCS and the Assistant Grade increased from 136.3 per cent to 151.4 per cent; this constitutes a substantial widening. One of the most discernible effects of the move to 'individual and differentiated pay' has therefore been a widening of pay differentials in the Swedish civil service. Such a development would have been anticipated for one of the motives for reform was to address the 'double imbalance' and to increase the pay of the most senior civil servants.

Table 4.6 The Grade Pay Structure in Sweden
(Percentage Differences in Pay from Assistant Grades)

	1993			1996		
	All Employees	Females	Males	All Employees	Females	Males
	(1)	(2)	(3)	(4)	(5)	(6)
HIGHCS	136.3	137.3	138.0	151.4	153.5	146.7
DEPTMAN	102.4	103.6	99.4	115.8	116.2	116.8
QUALAD	58.9	59.5	59.4	67.5	69.2	65.5
ADMIN	30.7	32.2	30.1	34.6	35.4	34.0
QUALASST	10.3	12.9	9.1	11.2	12.2	10.5

Notes: a.   Constructed from the coefficients in Table 4.3 where the coefficients are converted to percentage differences by: $(\exp(\beta)-1)*100$.
       b.   All coefficients are significant at the 5 per cent level.

Table 4.7 Reimers Decomposition of Average Real Pay Growth in Sweden

	All Employees		
	Changes in pay structure	Changes in characteristics	Total pay growth
	(1)	(2)	(3)
All Employees			
Overall	48.9	51.1	6.1
Personal characteristics	23.8	13.5	
Region	-20.1	3.6	
Department	12.3	-8.2E-3	
Grade	32.9	34.0	
Females			
Overall	37.6	62.4	6.5
Personal characteristics	30.2	11.5	
Region	-14.5	2.8	
Department	-1.5	-1.0	
Grade	23.4	49.1	
Males			
Overall	66.5	33.5	5.2
Personal characteristics	-37.5	13.2	
Region	-24.5	4.5	
Department	89.5	4.5	
Grade	39.1	11.3	

Notes: a.   Total Pay Growth is the real average growth rate of pay from 1993 to 1996 in percentage terms.

b.   The figures in the 'Overall' rows are the percentage contribution toward Total Pay Growth of changes in pay structure and changes in characteristics.

c.   The figures in the other four rows are the percentage contribution to the Overall differential by each of the four sets of variables controlled for in the regressions. The numbers contained in each column sum to the number in the 'Overall' row for that column. The sum across the two columns and all four rows will be 100.

Accounting for Changes in Pay Growth

The move to Agency bargaining in Sweden offered the managers of agencies the opportunity to change internal pay structures. The move toward 'individual and differentiated pay' might have been expected to change the structure of pay within agencies. We have already seen one aspect of this, the higher pay growth offered to the most senior civil servants. However, they constitute only a very small part of the civil service and would not therefore have a large effect on the general pay structure. In this section we therefore address the broader question, looking at pay growth in the Swedish civil service as a whole, we ask how much of the growth in pay that occurred over the period 1993 to 1996 was due to changes in wage structure and how much was due to changes is the composition of employment in that sector? To answer this question we use the decomposition technique proposed by Reimers (1983) which was discussed in Chapter 2 and detailed in equation (6) in that chapter. Recall that the method of decomposition employed takes all of the characteristics measured in Table 4.3 and distinguishes between that part of the increase in pay between 1993 and 1996 which was due to changes in the relative size of the coefficients on each of the variables (column 1) and that part which was due to changes in the relative size, the weights, of the characteristics themselves (column 2).

Table 4.7 records the results of the decomposition of the growth in average real monthly pay between 1993 to 1996 (column 3). Over this period the real pay of all employees increased by 6.1 per cent while men enjoyed a 5.2 per cent increase women received a 6.5 per cent increase. Table 4.7 reveals that almost half of the increase, 48.9 per cent, was accounted for by changes in the pay structure of the civil service, that it was due to the returns to the measured characteristics of the civil service work force. The remaining 51.1 per cent, was accounted for by the changes in the characteristics of the workforce itself. Changes in pay structure accounted for 66.5 per cent of the overall changes in pay for men and 37.6 per cent of that for women. Thus, there were more substantial changes in the structure of pay for men than for women.

Table 4.7 also reports the contribution of each of four sets of variables shown in Table 4.3. Three of the four sets of variables, reported in Table 4.7 are self-explanatory, those for Region, Department and Grade, but the fourth Personal Characteristic is less obvious. This contains all the remaining variables which are the age of the employee, the number of years they have been employed in the Swedish Civil Service, the number of years they have been with their current department or agency as well as gender and full-time.

From Table 4.7 we learn the following. First, that changes in the pay structure were the most important determinants of the growth in male pay between 1993 and 1996 and that most of this was attributable to changes in pay structure within departments. Second, that changes in the pay structure within grades were also important determinants of the pay growth of both men and women. Third, that changes in the rewards to personal characteristics contributed to the pay growth of women but not for men. Fourth, changes in the grade composition of the female workforce in the civil service were an important contribution to women's pay growth.

What then do we learn about the relative effect of pay reform from these facts? First, individualisation of pay makes pay more responsive to differences in the individual characteristics of workers. If the effects of pay individualisation are important, then there should be relatively higher returns to higher skills, that is the change in pay structure should be contributing a lot to the growth in pay. From the decompositions we see that this is the case for both genders, although the effect of the changing pay structure is greater for males. The grade hierarchy is our most direct proxy for the hierarchy of skills employed in the civil service and we see that changes in the skilled wage structure is an important explanation of increases in pay. The effect was once again more important for males with nearly 40 per cent of their average pay growth resulting from the changing pay structure of grades.

Delegation of pay bargaining would generally affect the interdepartmental pay structure. Since departments were able (within bounds) to bargain over pay independently, we would expect delegation to result in a greater dispersion in pay awards across departments. For Sweden, this had little effect on the average pay of women, but a large effect on the average pay growth for men since a very substantial proportion (89.5 per cent) of their average pay growth came via changes in the department pay structure.

Finally, we saw that changes in the regional pay structure arrested pay growth. This negative effect of the changing regional pay structure could be explained by the reforms in pay setting. If pay had previously been set to cover the cost of living in Stockholm, the costliest place to live in Sweden, then as pay became more decentralised and more responsive to local labour markets, this would have resulted in lower growth in pay, in the areas outside Stockholm, holding all other factors constant.

Conclusion

Though the analysis for Sweden is conducted over a shorter period than for the other two countries, Sweden is still a very interesting country to study. Sweden achieved the administrative and financial decentralisation essential for decentralised pay bargaining far earlier than the other two countries studied here. Moreover, the form of decentralisation it chose differed dramatically from the other two. It chose to set the ceiling on the amount available for distribution in local bargaining through centralised bargaining but to allow local bargaining to determine distribution within the ceiling. This system might have been expected to generate fairly uniform expectations about the size of pay award that would be achieved locally and to lead to little differentiation in reward. Indeed we noted that the intended individualisation of pay was far from achieved. And although we have no details of the size of pay settlements that were awarded locally we can evaluate their impact on pay. This reveals quite important and substantial changes within the short period analysed here.

Between 1993 and 1996 the civil service pay structure changed substantially, the rates of growth of pay differed substantially between the different agencies and departments and there was an increase in the dispersion of pay. Women's pay rose less rapidly than that of men and though the dispersion of pay increased slightly more than that of men, it remained below that of men.

One of the objectives of decentralised bargaining is to align rates of pay in the civil service more closely to those in the local labour markets in which they operate. It is therefore noteworthy that over the period the premium, the additional pay, for working in Stockholm rose from nearly 6 to over 7 per cent. Pay inequality also rose over the period. The differential for the top grade, Senior Civil Servants, over the lowest grade, Assistants, rose from 136 per cent in 1993 to 151 per cent in 1996. The pay of all other grades relative to that of Assistants also rose over the period.

However, the inter-departmental pay structure revealed little change over this period. There was a small increase in the dispersion of pay between the departments and agencies between 1993 and 1996 but as measured by the standard deviation this changed little over the period. The narrowness and stability of the inter-departmental wage structure is one of the striking features of the Swedish civil service pay structure.

The major impact of the decentralised system in Sweden appears to have been on the structure of relative pay. The most striking finding of this analysis was the substantial widening of pay differentials between all grades of civil servants in Sweden. Overall, the picture that emerges for Sweden is that the greatest changes in pay structure as a result of decentralisation took place among the most senior grades.

References

Andersson, P. and Schager, N. (1999) 'The Reform of Pay Determination in the Swedish Public Sector', in R. F. Elliott, C. Lucifora and D. Meurs (eds.) *Public Sector Pay Determination in the European Union*, London, Macmillan: 240-84.

Arai, M. (1994a) 'An Empirical Analysis of Wage Dispersion and Efficiency Wages', *Scandinavian Journal of Economics*, 96(1): 31-50.

Arai, M. (1994b) 'Compensating Wage Differentials versus Efficiency Wages: An Empirical Study of Job Autonomy and Wages', *Industrial Relations*, 33(2): 249-62.

Calmfors, L. and Forslund, A. (1991) 'Real-Wage Determination and Labour Market Policies: The Swedish Experience', *Economic Journal*, 101: 1130-48.

Edgren, G., Faxen, K. and Odhner, C. (1973) *Wage Formation and the Economy*, London, George Allen and Unwin.

Edin, P. and Zetterberg, J. (1992) 'Interindustry Wage Differentials: Evidence from Sweden and a Comparison with the United States', *American Economic Review*, 82(5): 1341-49.

Elliott, R. F. and Bender, K. A. (1997) 'Decentralization and Pay Reform in Central Government: A Study of Three Countries', *British Journal of Industrial Relations*, 35(3): 447-75.

Green, G., Coder, J. and Ryscavage, P. (1992) 'International Comparisons of Earnings Inequality for Men in the 1980s', *Review of Income and Wealth*, 38(1): 1-15.

Gustafsson, B. and Tasiran, A. C. (1994) 'Wages in Sweden since World War II- Gender and Age Specific Salaries in Wholesale and Retail Trade', *Scandinavian Economic History Review*, 42(1): 77-100.

Holmlund, B. and Ohlsson, H. (1992) 'Wage Linkages Between Private and Public Sectors in Sweden', *Labour*, 6(2): 3-17.

Holmlund, B. and Zetterberg, J. (1991) 'Insider Effects in Wage Determination: Evidence from Five Countries', *European Economic Review*, 35: 1009-34.

Jacobson, T. and Ohlsson, H. (1994) 'Long-Run Relations Between Private and Public Sector Wages in Sweden', *Empirical Economics*, 19: 343-60.

Katz, H. C. (1993) 'The Decentralization of Collective Bargaining: A Literature Review and Comparative Analysis', *Industrial and Labor Relations Review*, 47(1): 3-22.

Oaxaca, R. (1973) 'Male-Female Wage Differentials in Urban Labor Markets', *International Economic Review*, 14: 693-709.

Olsson, A. S. (1991) *The Swedish Wage Negotiation System*, Aldershot, UK, Dartmouth Publishing Company Ltd.

Pencavel, J. and Holmlund, B. (1998) 'The Determination of Wages, Employment and Work Hours in an Economy with Centralised Wage-Setting: Sweden, 1950-83', *Economic Journal*, 98: 1105-26.

Pontusson, J. and Kuruvilla, S. (1992) 'Swedish Wage-Earner Funds: An Experiment in Economic Democracy', *Industrial and Labor Relations Review*, 45(4): 779-91.

Reimers, C. (1983) 'Labor Market Discrimination against Hispanic and Black Men', *Review of Economics and Statistics*, 65: 570-79.

Robinson, P. (1995) 'The Decline of the Swedish Model and the Limits to Active Labour Market Policy', London School of Economics Centre for Economic Performance, Discussion Paper no. 259.

Schager, N. (1993) 'An Overview and Evaluation of Flexible Pay Policies in the Swedish Public Sector', in *Pay Flexibility in the Public Sector*, Paris, OECD: 113-24.

Statstjänstemannaförbundet (1997) *The Swedish Model*, Stockholm.

Swedish Association of Local Authorities (1995) *Collective Bargaining in Swedish Local and Regional Government*, Stockholm, Silby and Silby, AB.

Swedish Ministry of Finance (1995) 'The Public Sector Labour Market in Sweden: A Presentation', *Printing Works of the Cabinet Office and Ministries*, Stockholm.

Wise, L. R. (1993) 'Whither Solidarity? Transitions in Swedish Public-Sector Pay Policy', *British Journal of Industrial Relations*, 31(1): 75-95.

Zetterberg, J. (1989) Lönestrukuren och den 'dubble obalasen' – en empirisk studie av löneskillander mellan privat och offentlig sektor, Rapport till Expertgruppen för studier I offentlig ekonomi (Stockholm: allmänna Förlaget).

Zweimüller, J. and Barth, E. (1994) 'Bargaining Structure, Wage Determination, and Wage Dispersion in 6 OECD Countries', *KYKLOS*, 47(1): 81-93.

Appendix 4.1 Swedish Civil Service Departments and Agencies

Variable Name	Description
AGRI	Ministry of Agriculture
CULTURE	Ministry of Culture
DEFENCE	Ministry of Defence
EDUC	Ministry of Education
ENVIRON	Ministry of the Environment
FINANCE	Ministry of Finance
FORAFF	Ministry of Foreign Affairs
JUSTICE	Ministry of Justice (excluded in regressions)
LABOUR	Ministry of Labour
PUBAFF	Ministry of Public Affairs
SOCIALAF	Ministry of Social Affairs
TRADE	Ministry of Trade
TRANSPRT	Ministry of Transport

Chapter 5

The United Kingdom

Introduction

The 1990s witnessed a dramatic reform in the way that the UK paid its civil servants. The old structure of a small number of highly centralised agreements covering almost half a million staff was dismantled. In its place, a system of department and agency wage setting was introduced in which each wage setting unit had the flexibility to set its own rates of pay and establish its own grading structure. This move to a system of pay delegation resulted, in the words of one of the main public sector unions involved in this process, 'in an explosion of separate bargaining units' (PTC, 1996). It was a move moreover which was both conceived and implemented with very little public debate and which found many of its participants ill prepared for the changes. In this chapter we set out to analyse the first effects of this development on pay structure in the UK civil service. The full impact of such far reaching reforms will not of course be revealed for some time yet, but this analysis will report the first effects of the changes in pay bargaining systems that were made.

Private Sector Wage Determination

There were substantial changes in the arrangements for setting pay in the private sector of the UK economy during the nineteen eighties and first half of the 1990s. Both union membership and collective bargaining coverage diminished during the 1980s. Table 1.1 reported that in the UK, union density fell from 50.4 per cent in 1980 to 39.1 per cent in 1990 while collective bargaining coverage fell from 70 per cent to 47 per cent between 1980 and 1994. By 1990, collective bargaining coverage was estimated to be down to 40 per cent in the private sector compared to 78 per cent coverage in the public sector. These developments were in part a consequence of a series of labour market reforms implemented throughout this period which were aimed to increase labour market flexibility.

A large number of legislative changes introduced at this time sought to reduce the power of unions, reduce and eventually abolish minimum wage legislation and reduce employment protection (Millard, 1997 and Kavanagh and Elliott, 2000). Among the most important were the restrictions imposed on union closed shops and on secondary picketing, and the enforcement of secret ballots when a strike was proposed. During this period there was also substantial employer resistance to strikes, and governments no longer consulted union leaders over issues of economic policy as once occurred within the framework of the National Economic Development Council. This was a period during which unions lost a substantial degree of their power and influence in the UK.

During the eighties, the UK central government also sought to deregulate labour markets by abolishing the 'fair wages resolution' and Wages Councils. The 'fair wages resolution' protected the wages of public sector workers in low-paid occupations and the wages of workers in any organisation contracted to do work for central or local government. This resolution was abolished in 1980. Wages councils set minimum rates of pay in some industries in the private sector. They were independent bodies comprising representatives of employers and workers under an independent chairperson which were convened for the purpose of setting rates of pay and conditions of work in low-paying industries. These arrangements covered industries in which there was little or no union representation or where unions were weak. There were 26 of these Wage Councils remaining in 1993 when the government announced they were to be abolished although their powers had already been considerably reduced by the Wages Act of 1986.

During the eighties, pay setting in the private sector became highly decentralised. Although a small number of framework industry-wide agreements remained, most pay bargaining in the private sector now took place at the company level. There was moreover an increase in the incidence of unilateral, employer wage setting at the level of the company.[1] Perhaps in consequence wage dispersion grew substantially over this period. Table 1.4 showed that the ratio of the earnings of employees at the ninth decile to that of employees at the first decile increased from 2.78 in 1980 to 3.32 in 1994.

The Public and Private Sector Wage Structures

Studies of the wage structure in the UK public sector, and more specifically, central government have largely been confined to an analysis of wage differentials between the public and private sectors. The first studies used 'macro' data, sector-wide, or occupation or agreement-wide average wages, for purposes of comparison between the two sectors. Studies by Elliott and Fallick, 1981 and Elliott and Murphy, 1987 revealed that among public sector workers it was manual workers, particularly women, which enjoyed the largest premiums over the private sector. Research in the mid eighties and early nineties showed the importance of breaking down the public sector into the different subsectors of central and local government and public corporations, not least because of the changing composition of some parts of the public sector. Foster, Henry and Trinder, 1984 showed that during the 1970s, public corporations had the highest relative wages, while central and local

---

[1] See Brown and Walsh (1991), and Brown, Marginson and Walsh (1995) for details of these developments.

government wages were found to be very volatile. Gregory (1990) found similar evidence with consistently large premiums paid in public corporations, although looking at the differentials over time she found the government-private sector differentials were tending to become smaller. Elliott and Duffus (1996) investigated the public-private differentials by sector of government and disaggregated by occupation. Although they did not report the actual level of the differential, they tracked its movement over time. They reported a large decrease in the differential of between 5 and 20 per cent between 1980 and 1992 in non-manual occupations in local and central government, the National Health Service and Protective Services (police and prison workers). Only in education did the differential increase in a majority of occupations often in the range of 5 to 15 per cent. A similar story of declining differentials between the pay of manual workers in the sectors was found in local authorities and the National Health Service.

A small but growing number of microeconomic studies, using detailed survey data on the wages and characteristics of employees in different sectors were produced in the middle nineteen nineties to complement the aggregate studies. The first of these, Rees and Shah (1995), revealed that while for both males and females the public sector wage differential was positive, the male differential varied between 9.8 per cent and 11.4 per cent over the period 1983 to 1987 and the female differential varied between 22.3 per cent and 26.3 per cent over the same period.

A second study by Elliott, Murphy and Blackaby (1996) used data from the General Household Survey in 1983 because this year was the only one of those then available which contained a question on the sector of employment, a question on union status and comprehensive data on the length of the respondents working week – both paid and unpaid hours. That study again found a substantial female differential, 17.7 per cent, but the male differential was revealed to be smaller at 4.1 per cent.

The above two studies also controlled for sample selectivity and found that once the estimates were adjusted to control for selectivity relative wages in the public sector differed from those reported above. In the Rees and Shah (1995) study, the adjusted wage differential became negative for men and lay between -1.8 and -33.1. For women it was positive and fluctuated between 27.7 and 38.2 over the period. Similarly large and dramatic changes in the size of the estimated differential were reported by Elliott, Murphy and Blackaby (1996).

Disney and Gosling (1998) examined differences in public and private sector pay using the British Household Panel Survey (BHPS) and the GHS. They found that the public sector male premium, after controlling for the effects of age and educational qualifications, dropped from 5 to 1 per cent between 1983 and the early 1990s. The adjusted premium for public sector women, calculated after the same controls, on the other hand, increased from 11 to 14 per cent.

Blackaby *et al.* (1999) had a different focus in their study of relative public sector pay, they examined relative wages at different deciles of the pay distribution. Using quantile regressions and the Juhn *et al.* (1993) decomposition methodology on pooled 1993–1996 Quarterly Labour Force Survey data, they found strong evidence for the 'double imbalance'. They found that males at the lower end of the public sector earnings distribution were paid much higher than males at the lower end of the private sector distribution. At the upper end of the pay distribution they found that even though the raw pay data showed that, men in the public sector were paid more than men in the private sector, the authors found that this was due to the higher productive characteristics of male public sector workers. Indeed, they found that the public sector pay structure penalised males in this sector compared to those in the private sector and that it public sector male wages at this end of the pay distribution would have been lower than those in the private sector had it not been for the relatively higher productive characteristics of these male employees in the public sector. They found that women working in the public sector experienced a large premium at all points in the pay distribution. However once again they found that this was primarily caused by the relatively higher productive characteristics of female public sector workers.

Finally a study by Bender and Elliott (2002) estimated a much richer model, which controlled for a wide range of human capital, workplace and occupational characteristics. Distinguishing between manual and non-manual workers they found that as they controlled for more of the differences in the productive characteristics and the nature of jobs in the two sectors the differential fell. Before controlling for these differences males and females in the public sector enjoyed a pay premium of 9.1 and 27.0 per cent, respectively, compared to the private sector. After controlling for differences in characteristics, the pay gap dropped to 7.1 and 12.1 per cent for males and females, respectively.[2]

The evidence from the above studies suggests that during the eighties, women workers in the public sector in the UK enjoyed a positive wage differential over comparable women workers in the private sector. For males the picture was different, those at the bottom end of the pay distribution were paid more while those at the top were paid less than comparable workers in the private sector. This misalignment of pay structures, the overpayment of women and the 'double imbalance' for men, was one of the motivations for the reforms described and analysed below.

Developments in Central Government Wage Determination

The Organisational Structure of the UK Civil Service

A 1987 report – *Improving Management in Government: The Next Steps* – recommended the establishment of executive agencies to carry out the executive functions of government within a policy and resources framework set by departments. It recommended the creation of discrete management units as a means to improve management, recognising that changes in management could be

---

[2] In an alternative weighting scheme, the pay gap narrows still further, to 0.3 and 4.3 per cent for males and females respectively.

more readily achieved within clearly identified discrete units, headed by a manager with clear responsibilities and lines of reporting. A distinction was to be made between core activities, undertaken by the policy making departments, and the execution of these policies by agencies. The 'Next Steps Initiative' and the creation of 'Next Steps Agencies' and 'Organisations on Next Steps Lines' was the result.

A key feature of 'Next Step Agencies' and 'Organisations on the Next Step Lines' was that management responsibility was delegated to the chief executives of agencies. This allowed management to design organisational structures and associated processes which matched the tasks and duties set for their agencies. The distinction between core activities, policy making, and the execution of policy was intended to produce a clearer focus on outputs and outcomes, and on how best these could be achieved, in organisations with delegated responsibility.

The organisational structure that emerged may be illustrated by the example of Social Security. In 1996 six separate agencies reported to the policy-making Department for Social Security. Although 91,516 were employed in April of that year to deliver the government services which were the responsibility of this department, the department itself employed and hence was responsible for terms and conditions of only 2,750 of these.

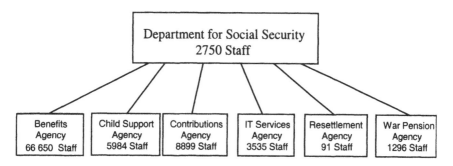

Figure 5.1 Agencies Reporting to the Department for Social Security in 1996

Figure 5.1 shows that the vast majority of staff working in social services in central government in 1996 were employed in agencies. A similar picture exists throughout the rest of the civil service and is reported in Appendix 5.1. In April 1996, the principles of Next Step Agencies were extended to all remaining government departments. The essential principles on which agencies and departments are constructed may be summed up as delegated budgeting and delegated responsibility.

Delegated Pay and Grading

Until the early nineteen nineties, pay and grading systems in the United Kingdom Civil Service were highly centralised. The vast majority of staff were in grades which were common across the service while centralised pay systems, with settlements negotiated nationally, covered grades of staff in all departments. In the latter half of the eighties, the government took the view that these centralised arrangements were no longer best suited to the variety of different tasks undertaken and services delivered by the civil service. Accordingly, it embarked on a program of delegating responsibility for pay and grading in line with the delegation of managerial responsibilities under the Next Steps Initiative.

The first steps on the road to the decentralisation of bargaining in the UK civil service were taken in 1987. That year saw the award of different size pay settlements to groups of workers who had previously been covered by the same negotiating machinery. Separate central agreements were implemented for clerical and secretarial workers, executive officers, senior ranking civil servants (grades 5-7), tax inspectors and scientists and engineers. Initially this increase in the number of central agreements led to some dispersion of pay settlements, but the imposition of a ceiling of 1.5% on all public sector increases led to uniformity of settlements in 1993.

The next stage was the introduction of delegated pay and grading into all those agencies with 2,000 or more employees. On 1st April 1994, 23 executive agencies covering over 300,000 civil servants assumed formal responsibility for the pay and conditions of their employees and in 1994 conducted their own pay negotiations. The largest of these were the Social Security Benefits Agency, Customs and Excise, the Employment Service and Inland Revenue. By March 1995, 15 of the 23 agencies had introduced new pay and grading arrangements and later that year they were joined by a further 13 agencies which conducted their own pay negotiations for the first time. In April 1996, delegation was extended to cover the entire civil service. The pay and grading of all middle and junior-level civil servants was delegated to departments and agencies, and the six national agreements that covered any remaining staff that had not yet negotiated separate arrangements were scrapped.

Each of the separate central agreements that existed after 1987, but prior to delegation featured a national pay spine which identified a fixed number of pay 'steps' for each grade covered. Under these arrangements any pay progression in addition to 'cost-of-living' increases was to be determined by performance. Upon the assumption of delegated authority, most of those departments and agencies, which introduced new pay and grading arrangements, replaced pay scales with pay ranges. Some of these ranges had performance bars designed to ensure that the stipulated maximum was only available to those delivering the very highest performance while some had fixed points beneath the band minimum for new entrants (see PTC, 1996).

A further feature of the new pay and grading arrangements was the restructuring and eventual consolidation of allowances. In October 1994 a single Recruitment and Retention Allowance (RRA) replaced allowances ranging from London weighting, a special payment for those working in London, to typing allowances. Even in those organisations which had not yet assumed delegated authority for pay and which were therefore still observing the central national pay agreements, this new allowance replaced London Weighting. The RRA allowance also replaced a range of other regional allowances ranging from the Northern Ireland Environmental Allowance, Skills Allowances and a Clyde Submarine Base Allowance. The main effect of the introduction of RRA was to remove entitlements from the pay system and replace them with a scheme which gave local management more discretion. The new RRA was not automatically pensionable, and it could be changed, reduced or withdrawn, should circumstances warrant it.

Delegation resulted in a further consolidation of allowances so that the comprehensive range of allowances and pay supplements which was a feature of the national civil service pay arrangements was transformed. The range of available allowances was not only much narrower but was no longer uniform between organisations. Some of the allowances were abolished while others were consolidated into basic pay.

The Individualisation of Pay

Even before decentralisation, a large part of the civil service and many agencies had some form of performance pay. From 1988, some 66,000 staff in the Inland Revenue Service were paid under a performance-related pay scheme, while middle and senior management throughout the civil service were paid under a performance-related pay scheme from around that time. By the end of 1995, 18 of the new agencies had introduced performance-related pay schemes, which determined the rate at which the pay of an individual advanced, for all or the vast majority of their staff. In most cases these new schemes replaced service-related, otherwise known as incremental, pay scales. These performance related schemes often strongly resembled those that has been negotiated in the early nineties for civil servants under the then existing central agreements and had two distinguishing features. First, satisfactory performance was regarded as a necessary condition for the receipt of any general pay increase. Second, the old incremental, service-related pay scales were replaced by pay spines, within which different pay bands were identified for each grade of civil servant and where progress up the band was determined solely by performance. The performance of each civil servant was assessed at an annual appraisal and although the new schemes for the most part offered the prospect of modest additions to pay, if sustained over a number of years, the additions could accumulate to comprise between 5 and 10 per cent of total pay.

However, initially the very speed of the move to delegate pay setting reduced the diversity of pay levels and pay structures that emerged. Agencies had little time to build the expertise necessary to manage pay delegation, and therefore many tried to cope by copying others. The PTC, a major civil service union, noted that many of the new structures copied those previously introduced for the higher grade civil servants (PTC, 1996). Moreover, agencies created networks of pay specialists to pool and discuss experience while they sought advise and expertise on the design of their pay structures from a very small number of pay consultants. Further uniformity was introduced because new pay structures had to be approved by H. M. Treasury who also monitored and approved the pay rises agencies proposed to award. It seems clear that these early days of delegated pay bargaining, assumed many of the features of 'pattern bargaining'. Thus, in the initial period of delegation analysed here, we might expect to find only modest increases in the diversity of pay structures and pay levels.

Contracting Out and Privatisation

While more common in local government and nationalised industries, some civil service jobs were subject to either privatisation or contracting out of services. These mainly affected lower level classifications such as catering and janitorial services.   One result of this type of reform was to make the civil service more homogeneous with respect to the grades it employed and the functions that employees in the civil service performed.   The impact of privatisation was primarily on lower grades, and therefore one of the effects of contracting out was to change the composition of civil service employment. There were now more higher paid grades. As a result there would have been an increase in average pay (since the jobs that were contracted out were at the bottom of the pay distribution) and a decrease in dispersion. These changes clearly run in the opposite direction of the predictions of the other reforms of pay determination. However, while these may have affected the measures of growth rates in pay or changes in wage dispersion, they should not have influenced the changes in grade or departmental wage structures that are estimated in the multivariate regressions below. Privatisation and contracting out will affect the composition of the civil service but will not change the returns to various productive characteristics of individual civil servants.

The Motivation for Reform

Some of the motives for the reform of pay and grading arrangements in the UK civil service have already been identified but a critical reason was undoubtedly the reform of the organisational structure of the civil service along Next Step lines. When managers sat down to design the organisational structures and the associated processes which would enable them to meet the targets that were now set for them by either their parent department or the government, they became aware of the central role of pay and performance management. A well motivated and productive staff were clearly key to achieving their goals since a majority of their running costs were accounted for by pay. Managing pay growth and its distribution was therefore understood to be essential.

A second motivation for reform of the existing pay structures was a desire to bring civil service rates of pay more closely into line with market rates of pay. The labour market context was one of substantial and growing pay inequality. The eighties witnessed a sharp growth in the inequality of pay in the private sector. There was also a general deterioration in the earnings of public employees during the long boom of the eighties although the evidence still seems to suggest that on average there was a positive public sector pay differential during this period. Though the process of competitive tendering had served to arrest the rate of growth of earnings of the least skilled in local government and the health service, it had little effect in the civil service where there was perceived to be little scope for contracting out. However, at the top end of the occupational hierarchy, the sharp growth in managerial rates of pay in the private sector resulted in a growing pay gap between private sector employees and those in the most senior grades in the civil service. Thus there was a need to devise a mechanism for bringing civil service rates of pay more closely into line with market rates of pay for the different civil service grades.

A third motivation was the pressure on public finances that existed in the early 1990s. This period saw the economy in recession, and there were, as a result, very strong pressures to contain public sector pay costs. This was in order to make way for some other items of public expenditure which would grow in the recession, namely unemployment and other forms of welfare benefit. While in the short term, costs were contained by ceilings on pay settlements instituted by the Chancellor of the Exchequer, undoubtedly the Treasury saw public sector pay reform as essential to containing pay costs in the medium term.

The above can be seen as the motivations for reform viewed from the employer's 'side', and they are similar to those we observed in Sweden and Australia. However, on the union 'side' there are two important differences between Sweden and the UK. The first was the 'enthusiasm' of the Trade Unions for decentralised bargaining. In the UK public sector unions opposed delegation having, for the most part, neither the organisational structures nor the experience to take advantage of delegation. The second lay in their power. Despite the high levels of union membership in the UK civil service, they had neither the power nor the will to oppose these reforms.

Analysis of Civil Service Pay

Chapter 2 detailed the source and nature of the data for the UK. The latter part of this chapter also provided a description of some of the features of this data, reporting in commentary on Table 2.7 the size of the gender earnings gap, the incidence of full and part-time working and the distribution of employment across the different agencies and grades. We noted a very large unadjusted, or raw, gender wage gap and a growing population of women working part-time.

Before turning to a detailed analysis of changes in the structure of pay, it is important to emphasise again an essential difference between the nature of pay reform in the UK and the other two countries studied here. All three countries experienced some form of individualisation of pay and pay delegation. The individualisation of pay would have been likely to make the grade structure more dispersed because the highest paid grades have the greatest opportunities to distinguish their individual performance and therefore the greatest opportunities to improve their relative pay. In turn this might have been expected to make the interdepartmental pay structure more dispersed. However because the numbers in the highest grades are relatively few it is not likely that this feature of reform will have had a major impact on pay dispersion. Pay delegation, on the other hand, could have resulted in greater dispersion because as a result of delegation each department was able to determine the size of its own pay award. Both would therefore be expected to lead to more dispersed pay in general. However, as we noted earlier, in practice in the early years of delegation there was a great deal of imitation, above we talked of pattern bargaining, and there was much less dispersion as a result of pay delegation than might otherwise have occurred.

In the UK as distinct from the other two countries, there was also contracting out and privatisation of some civil service functions. This would have led to a more homogenous civil service. While it is unlikely to affect the grade and departmental pay structure, it will change the composition of the civil service, leading to higher pay growth overall and to less dispersion in pay. Therefore, it will have an effect opposite to that of delegation and individualisation, on pay growth and dispersion, and so *a priori*, we cannot be sure in which direction pay growth and dispersion will change.

Pay Growth and Dispersion by Grade and Department

We start with an analysis of the raw data in order to obtain an understanding of the general magnitude of the changes in pay in the UK civil service. As with the other country specific chapters, we analyse changes in real median earnings.

Table 5.1 records these changes for the five main grades identified in Table 2.2 and in nine of the largest departments, which are detailed in Appendix 5.2. Table 5.1 reveals very substantial differences in the rates of growth of real median monthly pay across the different civil service grades.

Table 5.1 Real Median Monthly Pay by Grade and Department in the UK Civil Service in 1990 and 1996

In 1990 prices, £'s	All Employees			Females			Males		
	1990	1996	% Change	1990	1996	% Change	1990	1996	% Change
All Employees	715.91	839.34	17.2	692.08	793.76	14.7	969.33	1102.26	13.7
GRADES									
Senior CS	3068.17	3351.01	9.2	2978.42	3302.07	10.9	3068.17	3353.24	9.3
Higher CS	2096.67	2321.36	10.7	2096.67	2261.93	7.9	2096.67	2333.83	11.3
EO's	989.25	1126.87	13.9	989.25	1089.18	10.1	1009.58	1125.67	11.5
Administrative Officer	692.08	793.76	14.7	692.08	787.90	13.8	740.58	829.56	12.0
Administrative Assistant	546.17	621.90	13.7	546.17	621.78	13.8	546.17	621.92	13.9
DEPARTMENTS									
Agriculture, Fisheries and Food	969.33	944.40	-2.6	692.08	802.39	15.9	1242.42	1202.17	-3.2
Cabinet Office	807.17	1089.72	35.0	740.58	898.26	21.3	1212.42	1363.03	12.4
Treasury	930.79	1186.03	27.4	740.58	898.12	21.3	1164.08	1448.85	24.5
Custom and Excise	969.33	1059.12	9.3	692.08	821.47	18.7	969.33	1080.69	11.5
Education and Employment	763.50	793.76	4.0	692.08	793.43	14.6	969.33	913.18	-5.8
Environment	1095.08	1142.71	4.3	752.42	858.55	14.1	1643.17	1519.73	-7.5
Home Office	1296.17	1198.26	-7.6	826.00	862.46	4.4	1360.42	1302.62	-4.2
Courts (Lord Chancellors Dept)	692.08	793.43	14.6	692.08	775.70	12.08	740.58	868.33	17.2
Social Security	715.92	803.00	12.2	715.92	796.80	11.3	766.08	815.00	6.4
Trade and Industry	969.33	1014.82	4.7	692.08	802.39	15.9	1212.42	1256.58	3.6

Overall, the percentage change in real median pay was 17.2 per cent over the six year time period. For women, the increase was 14.7 per cent, while for men it was a slightly smaller 13.7 per cent.[3] The largest increases occurred at the lower grades for both men and women. Median pay increased by 13.8 per cent for female Administrative Officers and Administrative Assistants, while males in these two grades experienced increases of 12 and 13.9 per cent. This compared to between 7.9 and 11.3 per cent increases for men and women in the highest two grades.

The lower half of Table 5.1 details the changes in real median pay by department. The effects of pay delegation, the individualisation of pay and contracting out are likely to have had a significant impact on pay. Delegation meant that departments were allowed to set their pay levels and decide upon their own pay structures while contracting out will have changed the composition of the workforce. Both may well have produced substantial variations in the size of the changes in median pay. Though this is only the raw data, before introducing any controls through the use of OLS, the results in Table 5.1 show a considerable variation in the size of changes in real median pay between 1990 and 1996. Cabinet Office civil servants experienced the largest increase in real median pay (35 per cent), while real median pay for workers in the Home Office decreased by 7.6 per cent. The pattern is similar for women, while for men the largest increases occurred in the Treasury (24.5 per cent) and the largest decreases occurred in the Department of the Environment (a 7.5 per cent reduction in real median pay). It is clear that there was large variation in the pay growth across departments.

Changes in the dispersion of pay are reported in Table 5.2. Measured by either the standard deviation of pay or the inter-decile range, pay became less dispersed between 1990 and 1996 for the entire UK civil service. This appears to be the case among both males and females and in most of the occupational groups. In order to explain these differences between the experience of the highest and lower grades we need to control for differences in productive characteristics.

---

[3] Note that because we are analysing the median, the median pay for the overall sample need not lie between the median pay for men and women. This is due to the 'compositional effect' of 'adding' the two distributions (men and women) together to obtain the full sample. Thus there is no mathematical reason for the median to lie between the medians of the other two distributions, as is the case of the mean.

Table 5.2 Pay Dispersion by Grade and Department in the UK Civil Service in 1990 and 1996

	All Employees						Females						Males					
	Standard Deviation		10/50 Ratio		90/50 Ratio		Standard Deviation		10/50 Ratio		90/50 Ratio		Standard Deviation		10/50 Ratio		90/50 Ratio	
	1990	1996	1990	1996	1990	1996	1990	1996	1990	1996	1990	1996	1990	1996	1990	1996	1990	1996
GRADES																		
All Employees	0.475	0.381	0.949	0.954	1.103	1.077	0.430	0.307	0.943	0.958	1.058	1.053	0.473	0.408	0.915	0.923	1.076	1.061
Senior CS	0.137	0.171	0.990	0.984	1.020	1.030	0.110	0.153	0.989	0.978	1.018	1.022	0.141	0.173	0.990	0.985	1.023	1.032
Higher CS	0.365	0.365	0.793	0.976	1.028	1.027	0.365	0.177	0.977	0.974	1.028	1.025	0.368	0.161	0.793	0.977	1.028	1.027
EO's	0.326	0.209	0.947	0.981	1.059	1.050	0.256	0.165	0.971	0.982	1.035	1.033	0.362	0.223	0.930	0.974	1.062	1.045
Administrative Off	0.330	0.228	0.979	0.972	1.103	1.072	0.219	0.142	0.969	0.972	1.016	1.011	0.400	0.284	0.969	0.968	1.104	1.070
Administrative Asst	0.525	0.207	0.968	0.957	1.027	1.016	0.550	0.231	0.968	0.957	1.022	1.016	0.438	0.156	0.968	0.957	1.031	1.014
DEPARTMENTS																		
Agriculture, Fisheries, Food	0.490	0.481	0.910	0.927	1.106	1.106	0.364	0.381	0.946	0.952	1.089	1.086	0.476	0.509	0.899	0.906	1.080	1.091
Cabinet Office	0.546	0.551	0.942	0.931	1.149	1.124	0.413	0.448	0.949	0.951	1.112	1.118	0.618	0.598	0.899	0.907	1.125	1.119
Treasury	0.486	0.513	0.927	0.931	1.119	1.114	0.361	0.418	0.958	0.961	1.081	1.121	0.512	0.518	0.908	0.923	1.090	1.107
Customs and Excise	0.354	0.389	0.921	0.921	1.038	1.044	0.295	0.373	0.951	0.937	1.062	1.071	0.347	0.371	0.931	0.931	1.062	1.059
Education and Employment	0.548	0.291	0.939	0.964	1.070	1.053	0.587	0.248	0.933	0.964	1.068	1.047	0.382	0.362	0.946	0.959	1.062	1.078
Environment	0.657	0.484	0.903	0.923	1.111	1.100	0.625	0.395	0.921	0.956	1.082	1.094	0.496	0.482	0.883	0.906	1.070	1.078
Home Office	0.482	0.382	0.903	0.917	1.032	1.031	0.682	0.442	0.913	0.949	1.076	1.064	0.329	0.327	0.913	0.916	1.027	1.025
Courts	0.337	0.327	0.964	0.967	1.086	1.076	0.277	0.283	0.959	0.970	1.058	1.061	0.390	0.380	0.959	0.955	1.105	1.084
Trade and Industry	0.554	0.493	0.917	0.934	1.106	1.104	0.512	0.412	0.957	0.953	1.092	1.083	0.498	0.490	0.902	0.916	1.083	1.092
Social Security	0.293	0.297	0.957	0.950	1.055	1.049	0.252	0.263	0.954	0.957	1.049	1.048	0.344	0.356	0.947	0.940	1.069	1.070

The discussion earlier in the chapter suggested that the individualisation of pay might have been expected to result in more dispersed pay among the more senior grades, and it is interesting to note that this is indeed what we find for the Senior Civil Service. Moreover, we suggested that contracting out and privatisation would be expected to reduce dispersion, and this is again what we find for the lower grades where contracting out concentrated.

The reduction in the standard deviation of pay was greatest for Executive Officers, Administrative Officers and Administrative Assistants – a pattern repeated for both males and females. On the other hand, there was an increase in the dispersion of pay among both males and females in the Senior Civil Service grades, both experienced increases in the standard deviation of their pay.

As with the changes in median earnings in Table 5.1, there was a wide variation of changes in the various measures of dispersion between agencies. Employees in several agencies experienced an increase in dispersion – most notably the Cabinet Office, Treasury, Customs and Excise and Social Security, while pay for civil servants in other departments (Agriculture, Fisheries and Food; Education and Employment; Home Office and Trade and Industry) decreased in dispersion. Although changes in composition may be important here as well, it seems that decentralisation and individualisation of pay also changed the dispersion of earnings across UK civil service departments and agencies.

Regression Results

The next stage of the analysis is estimating the determinants of pay using multivariate analysis; OLS regressions. Recall that OLS is used in order to control for any changes in the composition of the workforce. Once we control for those changes, we can then identify changes in the structure of pay, that is, the returns to the variables such as grade and department, which are likely to have been affected by reform. Note too that this is particularly important in the UK where contracting out and privatisation resulted in important changes in the composition of the civil service workforce, which will have affected pay growth. By controlling for these changes in workforce composition, we seek to identify those changes in pay structure caused by the individualisation and decentralisation of pay determination.

The results of the OLS estimation of the determinants of pay are reported in Table 5.3. These results distinguish the impact on pay of the region and department in which the employee works, their grade, and their race, age, and length of time in government service as well as whether they work full-time. The coefficients from the regression results reveal that the adjusted gender wage gap was substantially different from the raw differential reported in Chapter 2. In 1990 men in the civil service on average, earned 3.1 per cent more than women (the coefficient has been converted to a percentage) but by 1996 this premium had risen to 6.1 per cent. The regressions also reveal that the pay of both men and women rose with age and that in 1990 peak pay was achieved at an earlier age than in 1996. Peak pay was attained at 40.4, 37.8 and 41.0 years of age for the all employees, the female and male samples, respectively in 1990 while in 1996 the corresponding figures were 45.0, 45.1 and 44.8 years respectively. In 1990 a woman at age 30 would expect pay to grow by 0.3 per cent in the next year due to the rewards that attach to the acquisition of an extra year of experience. By 1996 these 'returns' to experience, at age 30, had risen to 0.4 per cent. The corresponding returns for men were larger than for women. They were 0.6 per cent in both in 1990 and 1996.

Pay growth was also associated with the length of time the person had worked in the civil service. The coefficient on this variable can be viewed as the return to the specific skills and human capital that is acquired as a result of the increasing length of time spent in civil service employment. The number of years of service at which pay is maximised fell over the period from 23.1 to 20.2 years for women and from 26.4 to 23.3 for men, suggesting that this particular attribute of employees, the acquisition of civil service specific skills was by 1996, less highly valued and therefore less highly rewarded than in 1990.

The Regional Pay Structure

The regional pay structure is reported in Table 5.4. This takes the area coefficients from Table 5.3 and converts them to percentages. The South East of England is the omitted area and therefore the coefficients reveal the percentage difference in average pay between each of the regions and the South East. Evidently the South East was generally the highest paying region for most of the coefficients on the other areas are negative. However, the differences are small, generally falling in the range of zero to 5 per cent with the exception of Northern Ireland. Northern Ireland was the highest paying region for all employees in 1990 but fell back dramatically over the period until it was the lowest in 1996.

It is clear that once we control for grade structures, the age and service of employees there is very little difference between average levels of pay in the civil service in different parts of the UK. Moreover the regional dispersion of pay has fallen over the period. The standard deviation of the percentage differences reported in Table 5.4 fell from 3.3 to 1.5 for all employees between 1990 and 1996. This same narrowing in the regional pay structure in the UK civil service is evident among both men and women. It should of course be noted that the London pay differential will be larger than the south east differential because employees in London receive additional London payments. Here the omitted group was the whole of the South East, not just London, and this therefore obscures the higher pay in London.

Decentralised Pay Setting

Table 5.3 Regression Results for 1990 and 1996 – UK

	1990			1996		
	All Employees	Female	Male	All Employees	Female	Male
MALE	0.031			0.059		
WHITE	-0.031	-0.013	-0.034	0.027	0.020	0.033
AGE	0.023	0.014	0.022	0.016	0.013	0.019
AGESQ	-2.85E-4	-1.85E-4	-2.68E-4	-1.74E-4	-1.44E-4	-2.12E-4
GOVTEN	0.014	0.014	0.012	0.019	0.020	0.018
GOVTENSQ	-3.02E-4	-3.03E-4	-2.27E-4	-4.25E-4	-4.94E-4	-3.87E-4
FULL	0.355	0.317	0.489	0.011	0.014	-0.011
REGION						
Scotland	-0.047	-0.084	-0.008	-0.014	-0.037	0.009
North	-0.038	-0.067	-0.018	-0.010	-0.027	0.002[a]
Yorkshire/ Humberside	0.003[a]	-0.049	0.022	-0.007	-0.022	0.006
North West	-0.009	-0.049	0.026	-0.023	-0.034	-0.012
East Midlands	0.047	-0.012	0.069	-0.011	-0.028	-0.003[a]
West Midlands	-0.020	-0.048	-0.016	-0.015	-0.028	-0.007
Wales	-0.040	-0.065	-0.019	-0.025	-0.051	0.004
East Anglia	-0.018	-0.059	-0.010	-0.028	-0.039	-0.023
South West	-0.017	-0.041	-0.013	-0.022	-0.035	-0.017
Northern Ireland	0.048	-0.009[a]	0.029	-0.062	-0.060	-0.049
DEPARTMENT / AGENCY						
MAFF	0.108	0.021	0.176	0.035	0.014	0.074
CABINET	0.078	0.008[a]	0.136	0.046	0.023	0.073
TREASURY	0.078	0.005[a]	0.131	3.17E-4[a]	-0.011[a]	0.033
CUSTOMS	0.012	-0.038	0.050	-0.010	-0.025	0.019
DEFENCE	-0.255	-0.072	-0.445	0.054	1.26E-3[a]	0.113
DFEE	-0.022	-0.080	0.072	-0.019	-0.021	-0.019
DOE	0.144	0.007[a]	0.250	0.034	0.012	0.073
HEALTH	0.442	0.215	0.657	0.033	0.018	0.056
HOMEOFF	0.318	0.079	0.385	0.235	0.111	0.292
COURTS	0.026	0.013	0.036	0.009	-0.006	0.026
HERITAGE	0.110	0.012[a]	0.141	0.098	0.075	0.125
DTI	0.091	-0.003[a]	0.161	0.015	-0.019	0.064
GRADE						
GRADE1	2.185	-	2.114	2.253	2.414	2.256
GRADE2	1.799	1.914	1.721	1.942	1.988	1.957
GRADE3	1.592	1.692	1.525	1.780	1.765	1.799

Table 5.3 (Contd.)

	1990			1996		
	All Employees	Female	Male	All Employees	Female	Male
GRADE4	1.534	1.626	1.463	1.642	1.636	1.657
GRADE5	1.422	1.552	1.353	1.517	1.536	1.527
GRADE6	1.277	1.497	1.204	1.396	1.462	1.394
GRADE7	0.843	1.119	0.819	1.154	1.184	1.157
SENEXEC	0.656	0.817	0.686	0.892	0.903	0.898
HIGHEXEC	0.500	0.682	0.488	0.690	0.695	0.698
EXEC	0.442	0.525	0.406	0.484	0.481	0.490
ADMIN OFF	0.263	0.255	0.305	0.276	0.228	0.336
INTERCEPT	5.542	5.757	5.403	6.138	6.260	6.061
ADJUSTED R^2	0.572	0.467	0.694	0.851	0.807	0.867

Note: The omitted variables are South East for region, SOCSEC for Department / Agency and ADMINAS for grade. All coefficients are significant at the 5 per cent level except when indicated with [a], which denotes insignificance at conventional levels.

Table 5.4 The Regional Structure of Pay in the UK Civil Service (Percentage differences from pay in the South East of England)

	1990			1996		
	All Employees	Females	Males	All Employees	Females	Males
	(1)	(2)	(3)	(4)	(5)	(6)
Scotland	-4.6	-8.1	-0.8	-1.4	-3.6	-0.9
North	-3.7	-6.5	-1.8	-1.0	-2.7	0.2[a]
Yorkshire / Humberside	0.3[a]	-4.8	2.2	-0.7	-2.2	0.6
North West	-0.9	-4.8	2.6	-2.3	-3.3	-1.2
East Midlands	4.8	-1.2	6.2	-1.1	-2.8	-0.3[a]
West Midlands	-2.0	-4.7	1.6	-1.5	-2.8	-0.7
Wales	-3.9	-6.3	1.9	-2.5	-5.0	0.4[b]
East Anglia	-1.8	-5.7	-1.0b	-2.8	-3.8	-2.3
South West	-1.7	-4.0	-1.3	-2.2	-3.4	-1.7
Northern Ireland	4.9	-0.9a	2.9	-6.0	-5.8	-4.8
Standard Deviation	*3.3*	*2.2*	*2.7*	*1.5*	*1.1*	*1.7*

Notes: a. Constructed from the coefficients in Table 5.3 where the coefficients are converted to percentage differences by: $(\exp(\beta)-1)*100$.

b.   All coefficients are significant at the 1 per cent level except when indicated
        as follows: [a] significant at the 10 per cent level, [b] significant at the 5 per cent
        level.

The Departmental Pay Structure

Table 5.5 reports the inter-departmental pay structure.[4]   In this table we have
converted the coefficients on the department indicators in Table 5.3 into
percentage differences from Social Security. The coefficients have been converted
to percentage differences by: $(\exp(\beta)-1)*100$. The following departments were
included in the regression, but not included in this table: Defence, Health and
Heritage. See footnote 4 for further discussion.

        The top of Table 5.5 shows the premium (if the number is positive) or the
discount (if the number is negative) for a civil servant working in a particular
department relative to a civil servant working in Social Security, after controlling
for all the other variables in Table 5.3.   The results show that most civil servants
earned a premium compared to those in Social Security. Female workers in the
MAFF, Cabinet, the Treasury, DOE, Home Office and Courts all enjoyed a
premium compared to the Department of Social Security in 1990. In 1990 males in
all the listed departments had higher pay than male civil servants in Social Security
but there was some change in the relative position of workers in Social Security by
1996.   In 1996 female civil servants in the Treasury and Courts had relative pay
below Social Security employees and male civil servants in DFEE also experienced
lower pay relative to workers in the Department of Social Security.

        Although there was a wide variation in relative pay by department once
we had controlled for other differences in worker characteristics, there is little
evidence that the departmental pay structure had more variation in 1996 compared
to 1990.   The bottom of Table 5.5 reports two summary statistics for the

---

[4] In addition to the nine departments listed in Table 5.5, three other departments were
controlled for in the regressions in Table 5.3 – Defence, Health and Heritage. These three
were excluded from Table 5.5 due to potential biases that likely affected the coefficients
on these indicators. Defence: in 1990 in particular there were some extremely low earners
in the Defence department sample that caused the coefficient for that year to be unusually
low. *Health:* between 1990 and 1996, there were substantial changes in the composition
of the Health Department as some (particularly high paid occupations) were shifted to the
National Health Service causing the coefficients to drop dramatically (Table 5.3 reported
that the 1990 coefficient for the overall sample was 0.442 while the 1996 coefficient was
0.033).   Including these in Table 5.5 would have resulted in large decreases in
departmental dispersion, which would have been misleading because there are only a
relatively small number of civil service employees in the Health Department in our
sample. *Heritage:* in our sample, there were only 60 members of the Heritage Department
in 1990. While there was a substantial increase in employment in this department due to
its relatively small size in 1990, it was decided to leave this department out of Table 5.5.
It is possible to recalculate the summary statistics by using the coefficients found in Table
5.3, if the reader is interested in seeing the effects of including these departments.

percentage differences recorded in the top of the table. The first summary statistic is the difference between the maximum and minimum percentage differences, this reveals how the range of percentage differences changes over time. In each of the three samples analysed, all employees, and females and males separately, the difference between the maximum and minimum percentage differences decreased between 1990 and 1996. The second summary statistic reported in the table is the standard deviation of the percentage differences. This again decreased for the all employees and male samples, but increased slightly for the female sample. On this measure of dispersion, the interdepartmental pay structure for female civil servants became slightly more dispersed over the period.

Table 5.5 The Departmental Pay Structure in the UK
(Percentage differences in Pay from the Social Security Department)

	1990			1996		
	All Employees	Females	Males	All Employees	Females	Males
	(1)	(2)	(3)	(4)	(5)	(6)
SUMMARY STATISTICS						
Max. minus min. percentage differences	39.6	15.9	47.0	28.4	14.2	35.8
Standard deviation of percentage differences	11.6	3.8	13.5	8.6	4.4	10.3
DEPARTMENTAL DIFFERENCES						
MAFF	11.4	2.2	19.3	3.6	1.4	7.7
CABINET	8.1	0.8	14.6	4.7	2.4	7.6
TREASURY	8.1	0.5	14.0	0.0	-1.1	3.4
CUSTOMS	1.2	-3.7	5.1	-1.0	-2.5	2.0
DFEE	-2.1	-7.7	7.4	-1.9	-2.1	-1.9
DOE	15.5	0.7	28.4	3.5	1.3	7.5
HOMEOFF	37.5	8.2	47.0	26.5	11.7	33.9
COURTS	2.6	1.3	3.6	0.9	-0.6	2.6
DTI	9.5	-0.3	17.5	1.6	-1.8	6.6

Notes: a. Constructed from the coefficients in Table 5.3 where the coefficients are converted to percentage differences by: $(\exp(\beta)-1)*100$.
   b. All coefficients are significant at the 5 per cent level.

The results in Table 5.1 revealed quite wide variation in the changes in real median earnings. Why then is there little evidence of increased variation in the departmental pay structure? Section 4 of this chapter reported the three main approaches to the reform in UK civil service pay determination: decentralisation, individualisation and contracting out or privatisation. The use of regression analysis enabled us to control for the changing composition of the civil service workforce caused by contracting out and privatisation. We hypothesised in Section 4 that the individualisation of pay would likely affect the grade pay structure more than the departmental pay structure, because individualisation is likely to affect the relative returns to skills which are proxied here by the grade hierarchy. However because this has been controlled by the inclusion of the grade identifier variables (see discussion below), it is likely that the departmental pay structure is picking up the effects of decentralisation. That said, the system of cash limits instituted by the Chancellor during this period (see Section 5), and pattern bargaining by departments (see discussion on p. 127), are likely to have led to a reduction in the inter-departmental pay structure, after controlling for changes in the grade pay structure. For Table 5.5, this therefore means less dispersion in the percentage differences from Social Security. Thus, while decentralisation would theoretically lead to increased dispersion in the departmental pay structure, the institutional restrictions placed upon it actually led to decreased dispersion.

The Grade Pay Structure

Table 5.6 reports the grade pay structure where the percentage changes shown in this table have once again been derived from the coefficients reported in Table 5.3. This reports the grade pay structure in much greater detail than was available for either of the other two countries. Each of the five grades (1 to 5) which compose the Senior Civil Service are distinguished together with the two grades, Grades 6 and 7, which compose the 'High Ranking Civil Servants' group. It also distinguishes the Senior Executive Officer, Higher Executive Officer and Executive Officer grades, which together, compose what we hence called the Executive Officer grade. The percentage differences reported in the Table are the percentage differences in average pay from pay in the Administrative Assistant grade.

When reported in this detail it becomes clear that some civil servants are very highly paid relative to the Administrative Assistant Grade. Those in Grade 1 in 1990 received almost 8 times the pay of Administrative Assistants and over twice the pay of those in the lowest of the most senior grades, those in Grade 5. Salaries at this level are determined by the deliberations of the Review Body on Senior Salaries (SSRB). The SSRB was so named in 1993, previously it had been called the Review Body on Top Salaries (TSRB) and had operated since 1971.

The remit of the SSRB requires it to 'have regard to the need to recruit, retain and motivate suitably able and qualified people'. The SSRB attempts to do this by examining the pay of private sector workers doing similar jobs to civil servants in high grades and then recommends pay awards based on this comparison. Since the returns to high skilled occupations have been growing in the UK private sector (see Table 1.4), using comparisons to private sector pay to determine the pay awards to high civil service grades should lead to increasing differentials between the high and low grades in the UK civil service.

Table 5.6 The Grade Pay Structure in the UK
(Percentage Differences in Pay from Administrative Assistants)

	1990			1996		
	All Employees	Females	Males	All Employees	Females	Males
	(1)	(2)	(3)	(4)	(5)	(6)
SENIOR CIVIL SERVICE						
GRADE1	789.1	-	728.3	851.3	1018.3	854.5
GRADE2	504.4	578.1	459.3	596.9	630.1	607.5
GRADE3	391.6	443.2	359.7	492.7	484.3	504.4
GRADE4	363.9	408.5	332.0	416.5	413.6	424.4
GRADE5	314.5	372.2	286.9	356.0	364.6	360.4
HIGH RANKING CIVIL SERVANTS						
GRADE6	258.5	346.8	233.5	304.0	331.3	303.1
GRADE7	132.2	206.1	126.7	217.0	226.8	218.0
SENEXECOFF	92.7	126.3	98.5	144.0	146.6	145.5
HIGHEXECOFF	64.8	97.8	62.9	99.3	100.4	100.9
EXEC	55.5	69.1	50.2	62.3	61.8	63.2
ADMIN	30.0	29.1	35.6	31.8	25.7	40.0
Standard Deviation	*233.69*	*194.51*	*212.60*	*252.82*	*292.34*	*254.44*

Notes: a. Constructed from the coefficients in Table 5.3, where the coefficients have been converted to percentage differences by: $(\exp(\beta)-1)*100$.
 b. All coefficients are significant at the 5 per cent level.

Besides showing the large variation in pay across grades in a particular year and sample, Table 5.6 also shows that the variation in the grade pay structure widened between 1990 and 1996. Among all employees, the difference between the very highest grade, Grade 1, and Administrative Assistants increased from 789 per cent to 851 per cent over this period, and the increase for men is even larger.[5] Most other grades also show increases relative to Administrative Assistants. Indeed, the standard deviation of the percentage differences from Administrative Assistants increased for each sample from 1990 to 1996.

These increases could result from one of several different factors. First, if the SSRB had followed its remit it should have ensured that senior civil servants received the largest pay awards in order to match those in the private sector, for we

---

[5] Note that there were only a few females in a Grade 1 classification in 1996, which may bias the estimated coefficient for 1996. In 1990 there were no females in Grade 1 in our sample.

know that pay inequality increased in the private sector of the UK economy (see Table 1.4). Again, as we outlined in Section 4, one of the purposes of the individualisation of pay was to make civil service wages responsive to labour market conditions which were at the time rewarding the more skilled occupations with higher relative pay. We would also expect the general increase in pay differentials in the private sector, to be reflected in a widening of the civil service pay structure, an increase in pay differentials for grades in the UK civil service other than the top civil service grades. The increase in the relative pay for each grade shows that this was the case.

Table 5.7 Reimers Decomposition of Average Real Pay Growth in the UK

	All Employees		
	Changes in pay structure	Changes in characteristics	Total pay growth
	(1)	(2)	(3)
All Employees			
Overall	102.7	-2.7	14.2
Personal characteristics	45.0	1.5	
Region	-0.8	-0.5	
Department	20.4	-4.5	
Grade	38.1	0.7	
Females			
Overall	82.9	17.1	16.3
Personal characteristics	73.8	0.7	
Region	8.9	-0.6	
Department	-13.8	0.9	
Grade	-13.5	16.1	
Males			
Overall	146.2	-46.2	11.9
Personal characteristics	11.0	1.0	
Region	-5.6	-0.6	
Department	54.7	-24.9	
Grade	86.2	-21.7	

Notes: a.	Total Pay Growth is the real average growth rate of pay from 1990 to 1996 in percentage terms.
	b.	The figures in the 'Overall' rows are the percentage contribution toward Total Pay Growth of changes in pay structure and changes in characteristics.
	c.	The figures in the other rows are the percentage contribution to the Overall differential by each of the four sets of variables controlled for in the regressions. The numbers contained in each column sum to the number in the 'Overall' row for that column. The sum across columns of all four rows will be 100.

Accounting for Changes in Pay Growth

Delegated pay and grading, offers managers in the agencies and departments, assuming delegated responsibility for these items, the opportunity to change the pay structure and the grading structure. In the UK, unlike Australia which retained a central grading structure, managers had the opportunity to change both. In this part of the analysis we therefore seek to distinguish how much of the growth in pay that occurred between 1990 and 1996 in the UK civil service can be explained by changes in pay structure and how much can be attributed to changes in the composition, the characteristics of the workforce in the different civil service departments. These two elements can be distinguished by the application of the decomposition technique outlined in equation (6) in Chapter 2. The difference between the log of real average pay in 1990 and 1996 is broken down into that part of the change which is due to changes in the returns to the observed characteristics (this is called the change in wage structure) and that part which is attributable to changes in the characteristics themselves. Column (3) of Table 5.7 reports the growth in the real average pay of the three samples of civil servants in the UK over the period 1990 to 1996, revealing that the pay of all employees grew by 14.2 per cent, 16.3 per cent for women and 11.9 per cent for men over this period.

In the cases of both men and women, pay growth was almost entirely accounted for by changes in the pay structure (column 1). The growth in men's pay was wholly accounted for by changes in the wage structure. Indeed, changes in the characteristics of the workforce arrested the rate of pay growth in pay so that it was smaller than would otherwise have occurred. Among women, changes in wage structure accounted for over 82.9 per cent of pay growth.

Table 5.7 also records the contributions of each of the sets of variables in Table 5.3 to the overall changes reported here where the variables have been grouped in the same way as in the two previous chapters. The variables in the groups, 'region', 'department' and 'grade' are those titled under these headings in Table 5.3 while the remaining group, 'personal characteristics', contains all those not in the other three groups. The variables in this group are gender, ethnicity, age, length of civil service employment and whether the employee works full-time.

This table reveals that there have been major changes in the structure of rewards to grade, department and human capital. For the overall sample of all employees, the most important determinants of pay growth were changes in the rewards for personal characteristics (45.0 per cent of the total 14.2 per cent increase in pay) and grade (38.1 per cent of the total increase), although changes in the department pay structure were also important (20.4 per cent of the total increase). Changes in the composition of the workforce had little effect on the growth in pay.

For women, most of the increase in average pay was accounted for by changes in the pay structure and in particular the rewards for personal characteristics which accounted for 73.8 per cent of the total increase. Changes in the grade and interdepartmental pay structure worked in the opposite direction detracting from pay growth by -13.5 and -13.8 per cent of the total increase, respectively. However changes in the grade composition of the female civil service workforce were also an important contributor to pay growth accounting for 16.1 per cent of the total increase. It appears that over the period woman gained increasing access to the more senior jobs and gained an increased presence in the upper parts of the grade hierarchy and this would of course increase the average pay of women.

The story for male civil servants is somewhat different. The most important explanation of the increase in real average pay was the change in grade pay structure which accounted for 86.2 per cent of the total increase, followed by changes in the departmental pay structure which accounted for 54.7 per cent of the total increase. Together these two factors would have led to an increase in average pay of over 141 per cent! However, changes in the characteristics of male civil servant workforce acted to restrain average pay growth. Changes in the regional, departmental and grade composition of the workforce all detracted from pay growth and would have led to a decrease in average pay by 0.6, 24.9 and 21.7 per cent of the total increase respectively.

These results reveal again the effects of the reforms; individualisation and delegation led to changes in the grade and departmental pay structure, while contracting out and privatisation led to changes in the composition of the workforce. Male civil servants appear to have been affected more by pay reform than women. The effects of changes in pay structure on average pay growth are relatively larger for men than for women.

Conclusion

The pay structure in the UK civil service changed between 1990 and 1996 with the introduction of decentralised bargaining, the individualisation of pay and the contracting out of certain activities. Of the three countries studied here, the reform in the UK was in theory the most ambitious. However, determining the relative impact of the three different types of reform attempted can be difficult because the effects of decentralisation and individualisation of pay can work in an opposite direction to the effects of contracting out. In addition the imposition of cash limits by the Chancellor, and the adoption of pattern bargaining by central government agencies which did not have the expertise to bargain separately, serve to reduce the impact of the reforms. Decentralisation and individualisation should lead to increased pay dispersion and should widen the grade and interdepartmental pay structure. However these other three factors are likely to have led either a more homogeneous public sector or to more homogenous pay awards across departments and grades.

The results presented here showed that there were some important changes in the pay of UK civil servants. Analysis of the raw pay data showed a large variation in pay increases across departments and grades. The raw pay data also showed, there was some evidence of increased pay dispersion among the highest grades from 1990 to 1996, although there was decreased dispersion among other grades and departments.

However the raw data confounds changes in pay structure with changes in workforce composition; that is it confounds the effects of individualisation and delegation with the effects of contracting out. The results from the OLS estimations showed that there was a large change in the grade pay structure. Between 1990 and 1996, both the range and dispersion of returns to different grades increased. However the interdepartmental pay structure showed less dispersion over time, except in the case of females.

Further analysis revealed the relative role of changing composition and pay structure on the growth in average real pay. The changing composition of the workforce was not a strong factor accounting for the growth of pay for women, while both the changing grade and departmental composition of the male workforce would have led to lower wages for male civil servants. However changes in the grade and interdepartmental pay structure were important sources of pay growth for men. In the case of female civil servants, the effects of the changing grade and interdepartmental pay structure cancelled each other out.

From the results outlined above, we can see some of the effects of pay reform on the pay of UK civil servants. The significant widening of grade pay structure reveals some of the effects of the individualisation of pay. This reform sought to ensure that the returns to skills imitated those found in the private sector where these returns had increased. There were relatively few changes in the interdepartmental pay structure and although decentralisation would have been expected to lead to increased differences in this pay structure, institutional factors such as pattern bargaining among departments and ceilings on pay growth mitigated these effects. Finally contracting out changed the composition of the male workforce and this retarded the rates of growth of male pay.

Overall, the UK experienced large changes in the structure of public sector pay from 1990 to 1996. This occurred even with substantial forces which might have mitigated the effects of decentralisation and individualisation.

References

Bender, K. A. and Elliott, R. F. (2002) 'The Role of Job Attributes in Understanding the Public-Private Sector Wage Differential', *Industrial Relations*, 41(3): 407-21.

Blackaby, D. H., Murphy, P. D. and O'Leary, N. C. (1999) 'The Payment of Public Sector Workers in the UK: Reconciliation with North American Findings', *Economics Letters*, 65(2): 239-43.

Brown, W., Marginson, P. and Walsh, J. (1995) 'Management: Pay Determination and Collective Bargaining', in P. Edwards (ed.), *Industrial Relations: Theory and Practice in Britain*, Oxford: Blackwell, 123-50.

Brown, W. and Walsh, J. (1991) 'Pay Determination in Britain in the 1980s: The Anatomy of Decentralisation', *Oxford Review of Economic Policy*: 44-59.

Disney, R. and Gosling, A. (1998) 'Does it Pay to Work in the Public Sector?', *Fiscal Studies*, 19: 347-74.

Elliott, R. F. and Duffus, K. (1996) 'What has been Happening to Pay in the Public Service Sector of the British Economy? Developments over the Period 1970-1992', *British Journal of Industrial Relations*, 34: 51-85.

Elliott, R. F. and Fallick, J. L. (1981) *Pay in the Public Sector*, London, Macmillan Press Ltd.

Elliott, R. F. and Murphy, P. D. (1987) 'The Relative Pay of Public and Private Sector Employees, 1970-1984', *Cambridge Journal of Economics*, 11: 107-32.

Elliott, R. F., Murphy, P. D. and Blackaby, D. H. (1996) 'Pay in the Public and Private Sectors: A Study using the GHS', *University of Aberdeen, Department of Economics, Occasional Paper Series on Public Pay*, 96-102.

Foster, N., Henry, S. G. B. and Trinder, C. (1984) 'Public and Private Sector Pay: A Partly Disaggregated Study', *National Institute Economic Review*, 107: 63-73.

Gregory, M. B. (1990) 'Public Sector Pay' in M. B. Gregory and A. W. J. Thomson (eds.), *A Portrait of Pay: 1970-1982: An Analysis of the New Earnings Survey*, Oxford, Clarendon Press, 172-205.

Juhn, C., Murphy, K. and Pierce, B. (1993) 'Wage Inequality and the Rise in Returns to Skill', *Journal of Political Economy*, 101: 729-46.

Kavanagh, C. and Elliott, R., (2000) 'Economic Policy the Labour Market and Reward' in R. Thorpe and G. Homan (eds.) *Strategic Reward Systems*, London, Financial Times and Prentice-Hall, 63-80.

Millard, S. P. (1997) 'The Effects of Increased Labour Market Flexibility in the UK: Theory and Practice', Bank of England mimeo.

Organization for Economic Co-operation and Development (1994) 'Collective Bargaining Coverage', *Economic Outlook*, Paris, OECD, 167-91.

PTC (1996) 'Whatever Happened to a National Service', *Research Brief No. 1*, London.

Rees, H. and Shah, A. (1995) 'Public-Private Sector Wage Differentials in the UK', *The Manchester School*, 63: 52-68.

Appendix 5.1 Number of Staff in Government Departments and their Associated Agencies at 1 April 1996

Part A

Government Department	Total Staff in Post in:	
	Department	Reporting Agencies
Ministry of Agriculture, Fisheries and Food	6,101	3,892
Cabinet Office (including Office of Public Services and Science - OPSS)	1,062	2,629
Treasury	958	-
Ministry of Defence	64,608	45,250
Department of Education	5,045	35,282
(Now amalgamated with		
Employment Department)	-	-
Department of Environment	3,355	1,323
Foreign and Commonwealth Office	5,787	28
Department of Health	3,732	1,063
Home Office	9,448	2,490
Lord Chancellors	851	10,376
National Heritage	337	666
Scottish Office	5,131	7,695
Department of Social Security	2,750	88,766
Department of Trade and Industry	5,684	3,550
Department of Transport (DTP)	1,971	9,100
Welsh Office	1,928	211
All Departments	219,363	274,929
Plus Customs and Exercise and Inland Revenue	-	75,197
TOTAL	219,363	350,126

Appendix 5.1 (Contd.)

Part B

Largest Executive Agencies	Total Staff in Post
Customs and Excise	23,186
Inland Revenue	52,011
Defence Evaluation and Research Agency	11,024
Employment Service Agency	34,912
HM Prisons Service	38,009
Court Service	9,829
HM Land Registry	8,149
Benefits Agency	71,593
Child Support Agency	6,528
Contributions Agency	7,464

Source: Civil Service Statistics, 1996, HMSO, London

Appendix 5.2 UK Civil Service Departments and Agencies

Variable Name	Description
CABINET	Cabinet Office (including Office of Public Service)
COURTS	Lord Chancellors Department
CUSTOMS	Customs and Excise
DEFENCE	Ministry of Defence
DFEE	Department of Education and Employment
DOE	Department of Environment
DTI	Department of Trade and Industry
HEALTH	Department of Health
HERITAGE	Department of National Heritage
HOMEOFF	Home Office
MAFF	Ministry of Agriculture, Fisheries and Food
SOCSEC	Department of Social Security
TREASURY	H.M. Treasury

Chapter 6

Inter-Country Comparisons: Developments in Australia, Sweden and the UK Compared

Introduction

In this chapter we compare developments in the three countries, Australia, Sweden and the UK and attempt to distinguish differences between them in the evolution of the civil service pay structure. In the first part of this chapter we analyse differences in the pay structure in the three countries, reporting differences in the growth of pay due to experience and tenure in the government service. In this part we also look at differences in the grade pay structure, and report the structure of pay differentials in the civil service in the three countries. The second section looks at and accounts for real pay growth while the final section details changes in pay inequality within the three countries.

Method

The analysis in Chapters 3 to 5 was conducted using the country specific specification, by which we mean the analysis used the complete range of explanatory variables available for each country. However, as we explained in Chapter 2, some variables are only available for one or two of the countries and we could not therefore run the same specification for all three countries using all the variables available for each country. In this chapter we therefore employ only those variables that are available in all three countries to explain developments in pay structure. We adopt what we have termed the 'common specification'. This enables us to draw more direct comparisons between developments in the three countries. The variables available for the common specification are shown in Table 2.1, they are the age and gender of the employee, the length of time they have been in government employment and the region in which they work. We also know the department in which they work and their grade. In Chapter 2 we explained that we have coded these variables so that they are comparable across the three countries. In the following sections we evaluate, in detail, the differences in the coefficients that emerge from the regression equations using the common specification, in order to understand the development of the civil service pay structure in the three countries.

Pay Structure in the Three Countries

In the following sections we examine in detail the pay structures in the civil service in the three countries. We do this by comparing and analysing the size of the coefficients on each of the characteristics which are included in the three regression equations. These regression equations are included as Appendix A6.1, A6.2 and A6.3 reporting the common specification regression results for Australia and the UK in 1990/1993 and in 1996 for Sweden. They are reported first for all employees then females and males.

Age, Tenure and Pay

Table 6.1 reports the impact on pay of two important determinants of the level of an individual civil servants pay in the three countries; age, which serves as an approximation for experience – for the longer employees continue to work, up to some maximum number of years, the more experienced they become – and tenure in the civil service – for again up to some maximum number of years – the longer they remain in the civil service the more skills, specific to performing civil service jobs, they acquire. Wage structures in all three countries reward both these factors, and they give rise to age and tenure profiles.

Just how pay reform will affect the returns to age and tenure is not altogether certain, since the reforms could have changed the returns in either of two different directions. On the one hand they could have reduced them, since the reforms in both Sweden and, particularly, the UK sought to reduce the impact of, or remove altogether, incremental scales. Under incremental scales pay increased with length of service and therefore if these reforms were successful, we might expect that the returns to age and especially tenure (both related to years of service) would *decrease* over the time periods analysed. On the other hand, a thrust of reforms in all three countries was to make the public sector wage structure look much more like the private sector wage structure, since only then would the public sector be offering a competitive return. Age and tenure in the civil service are proxies for experience and specific human capital accumulation, respectively, and if in the past, the public sector underpaid for these skills compared to the private sector,[1] then the result of the reforms might be that the returns to both of these determinants of pay increase over the period. Table 6.1 details the age and

---

[1] This underpayment occurred among highly skilled workers in the public sector and resulted in the 'double imbalance' phenomenon discussed earlier. This phenomenon was shown to be particularly prevalent in Sweden and the UK. See Chapters 4 and 5 for more details.

tenure profiles and reports the years at which maximum earnings are achieved as a result of these two dimensions of pay structure.

Table 6.1 Part A shows how the pay of civil servants in the three countries grew purely due to the effects of, first age and then tenure, while holding all other measured characteristics of civil servants constant. Thus we see in Part A of Table 6.1 that in 1990 the coefficient on age was virtually the same for men in the three countries and as a result the percentage addition to pay was virtually the same in all the countries in that year. It was 2.5 per cent in Australia, 2.6 per cent in Sweden (in 1993) and 2.7 per cent in the UK. By 1996 differences between the countries had begun to emerge. In Australia the percentage was unchanged at 2.5, but in Sweden it had risen to 2.8 while in the UK it had fallen to 2.4.

How do we explain these developments in Sweden and the UK? Above it was argued that the returns might either increase or decrease, it depended on the type of reform introduced. These reforms could be aimed to either reduce the importance of incremental scales or reduce the underpayment to highly skilled public sector workers, perhaps even both, The return to age increased from 2.6 to 2.8 in Sweden and it therefore appears that the effects of reducing the underpayment were more important than reducing the impact of incremental scales. Conversely the return to age fell in the UK which suggests that on balance the thrust of the reforms in the UK was to reduce the role of incremental scales, and that this consideration was more important than increasing the relative rewards to highly skilled public sector workers.

There is more variation between the three countries in the coefficients on, and hence in the percentage additions to pay due to age among women than there was for men. For women in 1990 these were 2.9 per cent in Australia, 1.5 per cent in the UK and 1.8 per cent in Sweden. By 1996 they had reduced to 2.0 per cent in Australia, risen marginally to 1.6 per cent in the UK and risen to 2.0 per cent in Sweden. In these last two countries the returns from age were therefore very substantially smaller for females than for males. One general explanation for smaller coefficients and hence smaller percentages for women is that, in the case of women, age is a very poor proxy for labour market experience. This is because many of the women in employment, particularly in 1990, would have had interrupted employment histories, they would have spent at least some time out of the labour market. For this same reason it may be difficult to distinguish the effects of the reforms for they may be dominated by the effects of changes in the employment histories of women.

The impact of the number of years spent in government service on pay, the association between tenure in government service and pay, is also reported in Table 6.1. The coefficients on tenure in Tables A6.2 and A6.3 have again been used to calculate percentage changes.

Table 6.1 Wage Structure: The Role of Age and Tenure
Part A: The Percentage Returns to Age and Tenure

	Men		Women	
	1990[a]	**1996**	**1990[a]**	**1996**
AUSTRALIA				
Age	2.5	2.5	2.9	2.0
Age^2	-2.8E-4	-2.7E-4	-3.6E-4	-2.3E-4
Tenure	2.9	2.0	4.1	1.8
Tenure^2	-5.9E-4	-3.2E-4	-9.71E-4	-2.7E-4
SWEDEN				
Age	2.6	2.8	1.8	2.0
Age^2	-2.7E-4	-2.7E-4	-1.8E-4	-2.0E-4
Tenure	0.1	0.03	0.3	0.03
Tenure^2	1.5E-5	1.5E-5	-3.6E-5	-2.8E-6
UK				
Age	2.7	2.4	1.5	1.6
Age^2	-3.2E-4	-2.6E-4	-3.2E-4	-1.8E-4
Tenure	1.1	1.6	1.5	2.0
Tenure^2	-1.5E-4	-2.6E-4	-1.9E-4	-4.4E-4

Notes: a. All coefficients are significant at the 1% level.
b. The Swedish results are for 1993 instead of 1990.
c. The percentage changes have been calculated from the coefficients in Appendix A6.2 and A6.3.

Part B: Years when Pay is Maximised

	Men		Women	
	1990	**1996**	**1990**	**1996**
AUSTRALIA				
Age	44.6	46.3	40.3	43.5
Tenure	24.6	31.3	20.6	33.3
SWEDEN				
Age	48.1	51.9	50.0	50.0
Tenure	n/a	n/a	41.7	58.9
UK				
Age	42.2	46.2	39.5	44.4
Tenure	36.7	30.8	23.4	22.7

Notes: a. n/a – not applicable. This is because there are positive signs on the squared terms, and there is therefore no year where tenure is maximised.
b. The Swedish results are for 1993 instead of 1990.

In Sweden tenure has very little effect on pay and in the UK the effects of tenure are far less important than those of age. However in Australia tenure is important, it is equal to and sometimes more important than the effects of age. Where the coefficients on tenure are smaller than on age, this suggests that the length of time an employee has been in the civil service is a less important determinant of pay than general labour market experience. We also observe that in general the effects of both tenure and age diminished between 1990 and 1996 for the squared term is almost always negative.

To get a complete picture we also need to take into account the negative squared term on each of these coefficients. This is done by calculating the age and years of tenure at which pay are maximised. However before turning to examine the calculated figures it is important to clarify the interpretation of these figures. The age and years of tenure at which pay is maximised change as the coefficients on age, age squared, tenure and tenure squared change. It is easy to see that if the coefficient on age or tenure increases, then this will increase the age or tenure at which pay is maximised. The same is also correct when the coefficient on the squared term increases.[2] Therefore, if both coefficients increase, then the age and years of tenure where pay is maximised also increase. However when the coefficient on age squared decreases (i.e. becomes more negative), then the change in the age at which pay is maximised will depend upon the relative magnitude of the changes in the two coefficients, the squared and the non-squared terms, and this will also be true for tenure.

In Table 6.1 Part B we find that the age at which maximum pay was obtained increased in all three countries. The relationship between pay and tenure is however different in the UK. In particular there has been a fall in the impact of tenure on pay, although it is more pronounced for men than for women. In other countries there is also a dramatic change. The tenure profiles of Australian men and women reveal that the years of tenure that achieve maximum earnings rose by almost seven years for men and almost thirteen years for women. The profiles for Sweden have modest, but still positive, increases.

Together, the rewards for age and tenure in the civil service capture an important element of pay systems in the civil service in all three countries. The traditional mechanism by which pay was linked to age and tenure in the civil service was through incremental payment systems. Age and tenure proxy accumulated general and specific human capital, and incremental pay scales are an institutional mechanism for rewarding these accumulated skills. The thrust of pay reforms in all three countries has been twofold: the first to substantially reduce the impact of incremental payment systems and the second to increase the relative rewards for higher skills. As a result the reforms work in two opposing directions with respect to the returns to age and tenure. The reduced emphasis on incremental pay systems, lessens the impact of age and tenure on pay, offering higher rewards

---

[2] This is easily shown by taking the derivative of equations (1) and (2) in Chapter 3 with respect to each of the coefficients.

to general and specific skills will however increase the effects on pay of age and tenure in the service.

We can observe only the combined effects and they seem to suggest the following. In Australia, there was little change in the age effect and a decrease in the tenure effect and it thus appears that the move away from payments under incremental pay scales had the relatively stronger effect. The opposite was however true for Sweden, where the returns to age became more important and there was little change in returns to tenure. In Sweden rewarding higher skills was the dominant effect of reform. Finally, in the UK there was a decrease in the returns to age (for men) and an increase in the returns to tenure, thus the emphasis switched away from rewarding general labour market experience toward rewarding more specific skills.

Gender Differences in Pay

The raw differences between male and female pay were shown in Table 2.2. These values are reported in parenthesis in Table 6.2 together with the adjusted differential that emerges from the regression including all the controls contained in the common specification. Table 2.2 revealed that the raw, unadjusted difference between the pay of men and women in the three countries was substantial. It revealed that In 1996 men were paid 29.8 per cent more than women in the UK, 18.3 per cent more than women in Australia and 15.4 per cent more than women in Sweden. The raw difference in pay was found to be much greater in the UK than in the other two countries.

Table 6.2 Pay Differences between Men and Women
(The percentage mark up of men's pay over that of women)

	1990	1996
Australia	5.7 (24.5)	4.8 (18.3)
Sweden (1993)	5.7 (14.3)	6.1 (15.4)
UK	4.3 (35.0)	7.8 (29.8)

The raw, unadjusted percentage difference in pay between men and women is shown in parenthesis.

Notes: a. The adjusted percentage differential is calculated from the coefficient on the male dummy variable in the regressions in Appendix A6.1.
       b. The Swedish results are for 1993 instead of 1990.

However, the picture changes dramatically once we account for differences between men and women, in their age, tenure, and the grade, department and the region in which they are employed using the regression analysis. We see that the adjusted pay differential falls dramatically. The difference between men's and women's pay was greater in the UK in 1996 than in the other two countries but at 7.8 per cent it was considerably smaller than the raw differential had suggested. In 1996 the gender wage gap was 6.1 per cent in Sweden and 4.8 per cent in Australia. In the former it had risen over the period from 1990 and this had also happened in the UK, but in Australia the gender wage gap fell between 1990 and 1996. It should be noted that compared to other sectors and industries in these three countries, the gender pay gap in the civil service is very small indeed.[3]

The Departmental Pay Structure

Another way to analyse the changes brought about by reform is to look at the inter-departmental pay structure, which is summarised in Table 6.3. Where departments have used their delegated powers to strike different pay deals and where they have restructured pay and grading this is likely to lead to greater diversity in the inter-departmental pay structures. In this table we report two measures of dispersion of pay between departments, first the standard deviation of the differences in pay levels between different departments and the department excluded in the regression, second the percentage difference between the highest and lowest paying departments. The data used to generate these are the coefficients from the regressions using the male and female samples based on the common variable specification found in the appendix.

Table 6.3 The Departmental Pay Structure

	Australia		Sweden		UK	
	1990	**1996**	**1993**	**1996**	**1990**	**1996**
ALL EMPLOYEES						
Highest-Lowest (%)*	35.25	34.94	11.22	12.76	44.39	29.43
Standard Deviation[+]	6.73	6.34	3.20	3.52	13.90	8.71
FEMALES						
Highest-Lowest (%)*	31.42	39.24	14.11	16.03	26.20	14.75
Standard Deviation[+]	6.52	6.68	4.16	4.22	8.11	4.30
MALES						
Highest-Lowest (%)*	39.94	35.91	6.36	8.97	46.63	36.37
Standard Deviation[+]	7.38	6.62	2.02	2.58	14.95	11.00

Notes: a. * Percentage difference between the highest and the lowest paying departments.

b. [+] Standard deviation of differences in pay levels between departments.

c. UK summary statistics do not include Health, Heritage and Defence for reasons given in Chapter 5.

---

[3] See Blau and Kahn (1996) for cross country comparisons for private sector wages.

Table 6.3 also shows that, in each of these countries, there was very little increase in the dispersion of the percentage differences in pay between departments, holding all other variables constant. For all employees in Australia, there was a slight increase in dispersion as measured by the difference between the highest and lowest paying departments, but when measured by the standard deviation of the percentage differences dispersion fell between 1990 and 1996. The decrease in dispersion among all employees captured by the standard deviation reflected the experience of male workers, who on both measures experienced decreases in dispersion, for females experienced a small increase in dispersion.

There were large decreases in both measures of inter-departmental pay dispersion for both males and females in the UK. Only in Sweden did both measures of dispersion show increases for both males and females although because the changes were relatively small, there was relatively little change in the magnitude of dispersion of the interdepartmental wage structure over the period.

The summary statistics[4] in Table 6.3 reveal that there were relatively large differences between countries in the magnitude of the dispersion of the interdepartmental wage structure in 1990. Sweden had a much smaller dispersion of pay between departments than either of the other two countries: in Sweden the dispersion of the interdepartmental pay structure for all employees is less than one third that in the other two countries where the magnitude of dispersion is similar. The pattern is the same across the three countries for males only and, for the most part, women only but there was greater dispersion in the women's interdepartmental pay structure in Australia than in the UK.

In Chapter 2 we hypothesised that decentralisation should increase inter-departmental pay dispersion. However, we find that this happens only in Sweden (and for Australian females). So, why is this the case? In the country specific chapters we explained that there were other institutional factors that accompanied delegation of pay bargaining in Australia and the UK that would limit the size of any increase in inter-department pay dispersion. In Australia, the impact of decentralisation on inter-departmental pay dispersion was severely limited by several factors but the most important was the 'fold-back' mechanism which shared

---

[4] A comparison of the results in Table 6.3 with those in Tables 3.5 (Australia), 4.5 (Sweden) and 5.5 (UK) reveals that the Australian country specific results are slightly smaller in magnitude than the common specification but the change over time is similar. Again in Sweden the magnitudes of the country specific results is slightly smaller in 1993 in the overall sample and the standard deviation for women reveals a slightly different magnitude. In the UK the magnitudes of both summary statistics for women in 1990 are smaller in the country specific specification and the standard deviation increases for women. However the summary results from the common specification (reported in Table 6.3) are of similar order of magnitude and direction of change to the country specific results. This similarity between the two specifications, indicates that any biases that might have been introduced through missing variables when using the common specification (compared to the specific specification) are relatively small.

the results of the productivity increases achieved in some departments between all departments. Therefore, though there was dispersion among the initial bargained outcomes, the ultimate effect on pay was to produce a great deal of uniformity in pay increases across departments (see Chapter 3).

There were two factors which limited the effects of decentralisation in the UK, and these were reported in Chapter 5. First, the Chancellor of the Exchequer instituted cash limits on increases in departmental funding which effectively capped the level of increases in pay across departments. Second many agencies followed the agreements struck and imitated the outcomes achieved, in other agencies. There was pattern bargaining and this lead to greater uniformity in pay levels across departments than would otherwise have occurred. These two factors will have resulted in reduced dispersion in the inter-departmental pay distribution, as revealed by the results reported in Chapter 5 for the UK country specific data and specification.

The Grade Pay Structure

The Table 6.4 details pay differentials between the civil service grades in each of the three countries.[5] These differentials are calculated by expressing the pay of the most senior civil servants and the grades below them in each country as an index of the pay of the most junior civil service grade in the same country where this latter is equal to 1. In addition, we calculate the standard deviation, of the pay differentials between the different grades to provide a single measure of overall dispersion at a point in time. This then allows us to examine how dispersion has changed over time by comparing the start and end year standard deviations.

---

[5] A comparison of the results from the common specification reported in Table 6.4 and the results from the country specific specification reported in Tables 3.6 (Australia), 4.6 (Sweden) and 5.6 (UK) shows some differences. The results for Australia and Sweden both reveal that the differences in pay between the different grades are larger on the country specific specification than on the common specification reported in Table 6.4. It is more difficult to make such a comparison for the UK, because in this case we collapsed the very highest grades reported in the country specific specification into a much smaller number of grades for the common specification to allow us to draw comparisons between the three countries. But to the extent that it is possible it would seem that, as in the case of the other two countries, the differences in pay are larger in the country specific specification. However it should also be added that among the three countries it is in the UK that the measures of pay differentials are most similar between the two specifications.

We suggested above that there did not appear to be any systematic difference and therefore any bias between the estimates of the magnitude of the dispersion of the interdepartmental wage structure we derived using the two specifications. In contrast there seem to be more systematic differences between the magnitudes of the dispersion of pay between different grades derived using the two specifications. However, they seem to be working in the same direction in each country (making the differentials smaller across grades in each country) and we get similar results from the two specifications when we look at changes over time – namely that pay dispersion between the grades has increased in each country.

Within each country the structure of pay differentials between the grades is similar for women and men, but it is not identical. The dispersion of the pay structure, when measured by the percentage difference between the pay of the top and the pay of the most junior grades, was slightly greater for men than for women in Sweden, while it was greater for women than for men in the UK and Australia. More significantly there were substantial differences between countries. Differentials were widest in the UK and narrowest in Australia. Top civil servants in 1996 earned over four times as much as junior civil servants in the UK but only just over twice as much in Australia. We saw earlier, in Table 1.4, that the UK was the country with the widest overall pay differentials, and this is reflected in the civil service pay structure, even after controlling for differences in other characteristics.

Between 1990 and 1996 pay differentials widened in all three countries. In the UK, the pay of male senior civil servants increased from 3.9 times the pay of the most junior grades in 1990 to 4.7 times in 1996. The corresponding figures for women were 4.4 to 4.8. In Australia pay differentials widened from 2.0 times to 2.2 for men and from 2.2 to 2.5 for women between 1990 and 1996. Over the shorter period in Sweden differentials increased from 2.5 to 2.6 for men and from 2.4 to 2.5 for women. An increase in pay differentials between grades was, therefore, a feature of the civil service in all three countries.

Further down the grade hierarchy there are still differences between the UK and Sweden. Note the Australian classification of grades is different at levels 2 and 3 and therefore it is difficult to compare the results for Australia with those for the other two. The ratio of the pay of those in Categories 3 and 4 to those in the lowest grade is again higher in the UK than it is in Sweden and Australia. We have seen before that in the economy as a whole pay differentials are wider in the UK than in the other two countries, and this is reflected in the civil service pay structure in the UK.

All of these results are further confirmed by the last row in each panel of the table where the standard deviations of the percentage differences are recorded. As above this shows that UK civil servants had the highest dispersion of all three countries, and females in both Australia and the UK had higher dispersion than men. In addition, the data show that dispersion increased over the period of reform. For men, the standard deviation increased from 0.43 to 0.54 in Australia, from 0.54 to 0.60 in Sweden, and from 1.17 to 1.48 in the UK. Likewise the dispersion of the percentage differences also increased for women with increases of 0.54 to 0.62, 0.54 to 0.58, and 1.44 to 1.61 for Australia, Sweden and the UK, respectively.[6]

---

[6] An increase in the standard deviation of the percentage differences between each grade and the lowest grade was also reported in the country specific Chapters 3 to 5.

Table 6.4 The Grade Pay Structure

(a) Men

	Australia			Sweden			UK		
Common Grade	Specific	1990	1996	Specific	1993	1996	Specific	1990	1996
1. Highest Ranking Civil Servants	SES	1.95	2.22	HIGHCS	2.45	2.58	SENIORCS	3.93	4.67
				DEPTMAN	2.08	2.14			
2. Senior Officers, Senior Executives	SO	1.41	1.61	QUALAD	1.62	1.64	HIGHCS	2.35	3.17
3. Higher Administrative Grades, Junior Exec				ADMIN	1.33	1.34	EO	1.57	1.80
4. Mainstream Administrative Grade	ASO	1.10	1.15	QUALASST	1.13	1.12	ADMIN	1.35	1.41
5. Most Junior Grade – Reference Group	GSO	1	1	ASST	1	1	ADMINAS	1	1
Standard Deviation of percentage differences		0.43	0.54		0.54	0.60		1.17	1.48

(b) Women

	Australia			Sweden			UK		
Common Grade	Specific	1990	1996	Specific	1993	1996	Specific	1990	1996
1. Highest Ranking Civil Servants	SES	2.22	2.45	HIGHCS	2.41	2.52	SENIORCS	4.39	4.77
				DEPTMAN	2.03	2.16			
2. Senior Officers, Senior Executives	SO	1.58	1.79	QUALAD	1.61	1.67	HIGHCS	3.12	3.34
3. Higher Administrative Grades, Junior Exec				ADMIN	1.30	1.33	EO	1.66	1.71
4. Mainstream Administrative Grade	ASO	1.14	1.21	QUALASST	1.09	1.10	ADMIN	1.23	1.26
5. Most Junior Grade – Reference Group	GSO	1	1	ASST	1	1	ADMINAS	1	1
Standard Deviation of percentage differences		0.54	0.62		0.54	0.58		1.44	1.61

Table 6.5 Accounting for Real Wage Growth: Reimers Decompositions of Average Pay Growth

	Australia			Sweden			UK		
	Changes in Pay Structure	Changes in Characteristics	Total Pay Growth	Changes in Pay Structure	Changes in Characteristics	Total Pay Growth	Changes in Pay Structure	Changes in Characteristics	Total Pay Growth
ALL EMPLOYEES									
Overall	48.3	51.7	19.1	67.2	32.8	6.4	94.0	6.0	12.1
Personal characteristics	15.1	38.2	-	46.1	4.7	-	13.6	10.0	-
Region	6.1	2.7	-	-16.2	3.4	-	-2.3	-0.5	-
Department	-7.0	-0.5	-	17.3	-0.3	-	12.5	-5.5	-
Grade	34.1	11.4	-	20.0	24.9	-	70.1	2.1	-
FEMALES									
Overall	44.3	55.7	22.4	49.6	50.4	7.5	70.1	29.9	11.2
Personal characteristics	15.4	41.5	-	37.8	7.8	-	53.2	11.7	-
Region	3.1	2.4	-	-10.0	2.3	-	6.8	-0.4	-
Department	-4.1	0.1	-	6.7	-1.3	-	-8.0	1.8	-
Grade	30.0	11.7	-	15.1	41.6	-	18.1	16.8	-
MALES									
Overall	51.9	48.1	16.4	82.0	18.0	5.9	136.9	-36.9	11.5
Personal characteristics	12.2	35.0	-	28.0	2.2	-	-5.3	3.6	-
Region	8.3	2.9	-	-19.1	4.4	-	-3.3	-0.8	-

Table 6.5 (Contd.)

	Australia			Sweden			UK		
	Changes in Pay Structure	Changes in Characteristics	Total Pay Growth	Changes in Pay Structure	Changes in Characteristics	Total Pay Growth	Changes in Pay Structure	Changes in Characteristics	Total Pay Growth
Department	-10.4	-0.8	-	55.5	3.5	-	58.1	-24.2	-
Grade	41.8	11.0	-	17.7	7.9	-	87.4	-15.4	-

Notes: a. Total Pay Growth is the real average growth rate of pay from 1990 to 1996 in percentage terms, except for Sweden which is from 1993 to 1996.

b. The figures in the 'Overall' rows are the percentage contribution toward Total Pay Growth of changes in pay structure and changes in characteristics

c. The figures in the other rows are the percentage contribution of either changes in pay structure or characteristics for the particular group of variables toward Total Pay Growth.

More importantly, given the similar data used and common variable specification in the regressions we can examine the relative importance of the determinants of pay growth across countries.[7] In Australia, for example, the causes of pay growth were fairly evenly distributed between changes in pay structure, returns, (48.3 per cent of the 19.1 per cent growth in real pay) and civil service characteristics (51.7 per cent). In Sweden and the UK where the drive for pay reform was more concentrated, we find that changes in pay structure were an increasingly important aspect of pay growth. In Sweden, it accounted for over two thirds of real pay growth, while in the UK it explained 94.0 per cent. The same pattern emerges when we distinguish by gender; changes in wage structure were least important in the Australian civil service while they were most important in the UK civil service. Furthermore, the changing pay structure accounted for relatively more of the total pay growth of males than of females in each of the three countries. Indeed in the UK, male pay would have fallen had it not been for the changing wage structure.

The other rows in Table 6.5 distinguish the relative impact that each of the various groups of variables had on total pay growth. In Australia changes in the returns to the grades in which they work and in the returns to their personal characteristics were important factors contributing to pay growth, they accounted for 34.1 and 15.1 per cent, respectively. In addition changes in the personal characteristics themselves, at 38.2 per cent, were also an important factor. The changing pay structures for each one of the four sets of variables detailed in the table were important contributors to pay growth in Sweden. In the UK the most important contributor to pay growth was the changing pay structure by grade. This is perhaps unsurprising given the results reported above, for they showed that there was a substantial increase in the dispersion of pay between different grades in the UK civil service between 1990 and 1996.

A different picture emerges for the UK when we distinguish between men and women but in both Sweden and Australia the picture changes little. In the UK changes in the pay structure for personal characteristics, 53.2 per cent, and grade, 18.1 per cent, were the most important factors accounting for the increased pay of women although for men changes in the pay structure for personal characteristics

---

[7] A comparison of the results of the decompositions using the common specification, reported in Table 6.5, with the results of the country specific decompositions shown in Tables 3.7, 4.7 and 5.7, reveals that there are some small differences between them. Though the results from the common and the country specifications for Australia are in general very similar, in each of the three samples, the effect of changes in both the structure and characteristics of the personal variables are slightly larger in the common specification than in the country specific specification. The Swedish results reveal a similar pattern but also show a slightly smaller contribution of grade affiliation to changes in both pay structure and characteristics. Finally in the UK, the contribution of personal characteristics is smaller in the common specification while the contribution of grade differences to pay structure and characteristics is more important. The net result is that changes in overall pay structure play a smaller part in explaining pay growth in each sample.

were not very important. For men changes in the grade and departmental pay structure were the most important factors contributing to pay growth, at 87.4 and 58.1 per cent, respectively. The results presented in Table 6.4 revealed that by 1996 the grade pay structure for males in the UK civil service was more dispersed than it had been in 1990. This helps explain the relative importance of the contribution of grade pay structure to pay growth. In contrast changes in the composition of the grade structure of the male civil service and in the distribution across departments would have reduced male pay growth, for they contributed -15.4 per cent and -24.2 per cent, respectively to the growth in male pay.

Real Wage Growth

The preceding pages have outlined how the pay structure in these three countries changed during the early nineteen nineties as a result of the pay reforms instituted by the central governments in these countries. Although there is a good deal of evidence that pay structure has changed, the effects of these changes on overall growth in civil service pay are hard to judge by just looking at the coefficients estimated from the regressions. To reveal the impact that the changes in pay structure had on the average increase in wages across the three countries, we decompose average pay growth into that part which can be attributed to changes in the composition (the characteristics) of the civil service workforce and into that part which results from changes in the pay structure. Furthermore, we decompose each of these two elements into their constituent parts: personal characteristics, region, department, and grade. Table 6.5 records the results of these decompositions.

The magnitude of total pay growth shown in Table 6.5 is similar to that reported in the country specific chapters (see Tables 3.7, 4.7 and 5.7). Pay growth is shown to be greatest in Australia (19.1 per cent for the overall sample), which had the most modest reforms of the three countries. Pay growth in Sweden was slower than in Australia, when extrapolated over a comparable 6-year period, but was slightly greater than in the UK. Pay reform was most dramatic in the UK, but there were institutional factors that reduced pay growth.[8] Females in Australia and Sweden had greater pay growth than males in those countries while there was little difference in pay growth between the genders in the UK.

---

[8] The Swedish data covers only half the period of the other two countries, we therefore extrapolated the real pay growth shown in the Swedish data to a comparable period to that of the other two counties. The extrapolated real pay growth is 12.8, 15.0 and 11.8 per cent for the overall, female and male samples, respectively.

Conclusion: The Effects of Pay Reform

Pay reform in the public sector was predicted to have a number of effects on the pay structure of civil servants in Australia, Sweden and the UK. The main thrust of the reforms in all three countries was to decentralise pay bargaining and, in UK in particular, to tie pay to performance – to individualise pay. The implementation of these reforms assumed a number of forms. First a reduced emphasis on incremental scales which would mean that length of service would become a less important determinant of pay. Second making public sector wage structures more responsive to the labour market and therefore more like those in the private sector. One consequence of this was that they would need to offer higher pay to more highly skilled workers, and this would likely increase both the returns to length of service and the relative pay of higher level occupations. Third the decentralisation of bargaining would likely increase the dispersion of pay across departments and agencies.

However other factors, features of both the reforms themselves and the economic circumstances of the time, muted these effects. Thus in Australia the 'fold-back' mechanism resulted in highly similar pay increases across all APS workers. While in the UK the introduction of cash limits and the practice of pattern bargaining across departments also reduce the diversity of pay increases.

We analysed individual civil service pay records from each country in order to distinguish the empirical effects of pay reform. We used several different methods in order to see how pay structures were changed by the pay reforms. First we analysed changes in average pay levels and in the dispersion of pay across departments and grades. However such a comparison of 'raw' averages takes no account of differences in the productive characteristics of the civil servants that are being compared and so we used multivariate regression techniques to further distinguish the effects of the reforms. We used this method to distinguish changes in the inter-departmental and inter-grade pay structures, as well as the returns to age and tenure. Finally, we examined two different regression specifications for each country. In the first we exploited all the detail that were available in a particular country's civil service pay data, we called this the 'country specific' specification. In the second we parsed the specification, in order to make the data sets as similar as possible and to allow us to draw comparisons across countries, this was called the 'common specification'. A preliminary issue was a robustness check to see how different the results were when moving from the country specific specification to the common specification. In general the same pattern of results was found in the country specific specification as in the common specification. The major results are reported below.

The effects of pay reform were expected to be most pronounced in the UK, the country in which there had been the most extensive changes. In the UK there had been the introduction of delegated pay, the individualisation of pay, and contracting out. There were significant changes in the pay structure in the UK, relative to those that occurred in the other countries and this was particularly evident in the changing grade pay structure. In 1990 Civil servants in the UK already had the most dispersed grade pay structure of the three countries, and over the period to 1996 they experienced a large increase in the dispersion of the grade pay structure. Although the decentralisation of pay bargaining may have contributed to this widening because it allowed the same grade to be paid at different levels according to the department in which they worked, it is more likely due to the individualisation of pay for the most senior grades.

A less clear result was the effect of pay reform on the departmental pay structure. We might expect devolved pay bargaining to cause the dispersion of departmental pay differences to increase. In our results we found that this is the case only for the Swedish civil service. For the other two countries, factors such as the 'fold-back' pool in Australia and cash limits and pattern bargaining in the UK reduced the dispersion of the inter-departmental pay structures.

Pay reform affected other aspects of the pay structure as well as those discussed above. The pay gap between males and females decreased in Australia, but increased in Sweden and the UK. This is likely one consequence of pay reform, because the pay gap between men and women is greater in the private sector and if pay reform moves the public sector wage structure closer to that in the private sector then the gender differential will grow. We also observed that age and tenure profiles changed, again appearing to become more like the age and tenure profiles in the private sectors of these countries.

Finally, we found that pay reform had different effects on the male and female pay structures. The pay structures for each gender are different in the private sectors of these countries and thus we should expect reform to increase the differences between the genders in the civil service. In general, it was in the inter-departmental and inter-grade pay structures that we found the biggest differences, with dispersion in the inter-departmental pay structure greatest for men and in the inter-grade pay structure greatest for women.

In the early 1990s, pay reform in the civil service was an important political and economic force in Australia, Sweden and the UK. The results presented here confirm that the initial impact of these reforms resulted in dramatic changes in the pay structure in the civil services of these countries. We would expect that these differences would become more pronounced over the subsequent years and that there will have been further changes if the reforms continued to be the focal point of pay policy for the central governments of these countries.

References

Blau, F. D. and Kahn, L. M. (1996) 'International Differences in Male Wage Inequality: Institutions versus Market Forces', *Journal of Political Economy*, 104(4): 791-836.

Appendix 6.1 'Common Specification' Regression Results for All Civil Servants in 1990/3 and 1996

	Australia			Sweden			UK	
	1990	1996		1993	1996		1990	1996
Constant	7.077	7.106	Constant	8.902	8.900	INTERCEP	5.827	5.984
MALE	0.055	0.047	MALE	0.055	0.059	MALE	0.042	0.075
TENURE	0.033	0.019	TENGOVI	0.002	7.8E-5 [a]	GOVTEN	0.013	0.019
TENURESQ	-6.9E-4	-3.0E-4	TEN2GOV	-1.1E-5	6.3E-6 [a]	GOVTENSQ	-2.5E-4	-3.1E-4
AGE	0.025	0.022	AGE	0.022	0.024	AGE	0.024	0.019
AGESQ	-2.9E-4	-2.4E-4	AGESQ	-2.3E-4	-2.4E-4	AGESQ	-2.9E-4	-2.1E-4
Region								
NSW	-0.109	-0.101	SOUTH	-0.066	-0.083	SCOTLAND	-0.028	-0.018
VIC	-0.109	-0.096	CENTRAL	-0.058	-0.079	NORTH	-0.038	-0.010
QLD	-0.118	-0.105	NORTH	-0.063	-0.066	YORKHUM	0.004 [a]	-0.003
SA	-0.109	-0.084	-	-	-	NW	-0.008	-0.020
WA	-0.142	-0.100	-	-	-	EMIDLAND	0.050	-0.019
TAS	-0.120	-0.100	-	-	-	WMIDLAND	-0.020	-0.018
NT	-0.074	-0.064	-	-	-	WALES	-0.039	-0.022
-	-	-	-	-	-	EANGLIA	-0.018	-0.030
-	-	-	-	-	-	SW	-0.023	-0.025
-	-	-	-	-	-	NI	0.035	-0.062
Departments/Agencies								
AIPO	-0.131	-0.107	FORAFF	-0.009	0.034	MAFF	0.139	0.017
ACCC	-0.053	-0.105	DEFENCE	0.066	0.091	CABINET	0.101	0.073
PSMPC	-0.068	-0.093	SOCIALAF	0.056	0.072	TREASURY	0.105	0.088
AIDAB	-0.025	-0.062	TRANSPRT	0.011	0.024	CUSTOMS	0.039	0.022
AGPS	-0.103	-0.117	FINANCE	0.040	0.041	DEFENSE	-0.238	0.081
AWM	-0.104	-0.117	AGRI	-0.044	0.052	DOE	0.233	0.112
NCA	0.034	0.050	LABOUR	0.019	0.028	HEALTH	0.523	0.073
AGSO	-0.119	-0.018 [a]	CULTURE	-0.012	-0.032	HOMEOFF	0.385	0.247
NLA	-0.197	-0.156	TRADE	0.031	0.009	COURTS	0.025	0.027
PMC	-0.025	-0.061	PUBAFF	0.008	0.011	HERITAGE	0.153	0.122
ANAO	0.037	-0.058	ENVIRON	0.036	-0.010 [a]	DTI	0.129	0.074
DVA	-0.064	-0.094	-	-	-	-	-	-
WEATHER	-0.128	-0.104	-	-	-	-	-	-
AEC	-0.018 [a]	-0.065	-	-	-	-	-	-
DSS	-0.097	-0.096	-	-	-	-	-	-
ARCHIVES	-0.054	-0.117	-	-	-	-	-	-
INDCOM	-0.067	-0.057	-	-	-	-	-	-
TREASURY	-0.065	-0.070	-	-	-	-	-	-
DPP	0.118	0.088	-	-	-	-	-	-
COMSUPER	-0.131	-0.173	-	-	-	-	-	-
ABS	-0.076	-0.106	-	-	-	-	-	-
CUSTOMS	-0.258	-0.290	-	-	-	-	-	-
ATO	-0.036	-0.063	-	-	-	-	-	-
DEFENCE	-0.101	-0.105	-	-	-	-	-	-
FINANCE	-0.044	-0.064	-	-	-	-	-	-
HEALTH	0.096	0.093	-	-	-	-	-	-
ANCA	-0.041	-0.074	-	-	-	-	-	-
DIR	-0.014 [a]	-0.053	-	-	-	-	-	-
DEETYA	-0.049	-0.045	-	-	-	-	-	-
DPIE	-0.111	-0.133	-	-	-	-	-	-
DFAT	-0.109	-0.109	-	-	-	-	-	-

Appendix 6.1 (Contd.)

	Australia			Sweden			UK	
	1990	1996		1993	1996		1990	1996
ADMIN	-0.051	-0.054	-	-	-	-	-	-
DIMA	-0.041	-0.057	-	-	-	-	-	-
ABARE	-0.069	-0.115	-	-	-	-	-	-
ISC	-0.010 [a]	-0.072 [a]	-	-	-	-	-	-
COMCARE	-0.010 [a]	-0.072	-	-	-	-	-	-
Grades								
SES	0.682	0.805	HIGHCS	0.887	0.941	SENIORCS	1.403	1.533
SO	0.354	0.487	DEPTMAN	0.722	0.763	HIGHCS	0.871	1.153
ASO	0.080	0.129	QUALAD	0.477	0.520	EO	0.436	0.563
OTHER	0.323	0.375	ADMIN	0.275	0.289	ADMIN	0.229	0.285
-	-	-	QUALASST	0.102	0.105	-	-	-

Notes: a. The omitted variables are the ACT, the Attorney General Department and the GSO Grade.

b. The omitted variables are the STOCKHOLM region, the JUSTICE Department and ASSISTANT Grade.

c. The omitted variables are the South East region, the SOCSER Department and the ADMINAS grade.

d. All variables are significant at the 5 per cent level, except where noted by [a].

Appendix 6.2 'Common Specification' Regression Results for Female Civil Servants in 1990/3 and 1996

	Australia			Sweden			UK	
	1990	1996		1993	1996		1990	1996
Constant	6.926	7.219	Constant	8.977	8.991	INTERCEP	6.014	6.129
TENURE	0.040	0.018	TENGOVI	0.003	3.3E-4	GOVTEN	0.015	0.020
TENURESQ	-9.7E-4	-2.7E-4	TEN2GOV	-3.6E-5	-2.8E-6	GOVTENSQ	-3.2E-4	-4.4E-4
AGE	0.029	0.020	AGE	0.018	0.020	AGE	0.015	0.016
AGESQ	-3.6E-4	-2.3E-4	AGESQ	-1.8E-4	-2.0E-4	AGESQ	-1.9E-4	-1.8E-4
Region								
NSW	-0.094	-0.089	SOUTH	-0.052	-0.064	SCOTLAND	-0.049	-0.039
VIC	-0.103	-0.101	CENTRAL	-0.050	-0.066	NORTH	-0.061	-0.026
QLD	-0.108	-0.097	NORTH	-0.049	-0.052	YORKHUM	-0.039	-0.018
SA	-0.111	-0.086	-	-	-	NW	-0.045	-0.035
WA	-0.109	-0.098	-	-	-	EMIDLAND	0.003[a]	-0.039
TAS	-0.119	-0.088	-	-	-	WMIDLAND	-0.046	-0.031
NT	-0.060	-0.044	-	-	-	WALES	-0.058	-0.040
-	-	-	-	-	-	EANGLIA	-0.054	-0.044
-	-	-	-	-	-	SW	-0.042	-0.037
-	-	-	-	-	-	NI	-0.020	-0.044
Departments/Agencies								
AIPO	-0.074	-0.096	FORAFF	0.003[a]	0.038	MAFF	0.034	0.020
ACCC	-0.061	-0.177	DEFENCE	0.050	0.068	CABINET	0.025	0.044
PSMPC	-0.093	-0.062	SOCIALAF	0.063	0.087	TREASURY	0.024	0.050
AIDAB	0.021[a]	0.007[a]	TRANSPRT	0.025	0.041	CUSTOMS	-0.018	0.003[a]
AGPS	-0.093	-0.069	FINANCE	0.041	0.040	DEFENSE	-0.060	0.015
ATSIC	0.019[a]	1.4E-3[a]	EDUC	0.064	0.066	DFEE	0.032	-0.018
AWM	-0.050[a]	-0.047[a]	AGRI	0.029	0.059	DOE	0.126	0.063
NCA	-0.005[a]	0.023[a]	LABOUR	0.050	0.053	HEALTH	0.319	0.044
AGSO	-0.155	-0.033[a]	CULTURE	0.018	0.002[a]	HOMEOFF	0.219	0.122
NLA	-0.182	-0.131	TRADE	0.019	0.034	COURTS	0.007	0.010
PMC	-0.005[a]	-0.041	PUBAFF	0.017	0.017	HERITAGE	0.062[a]	0.109
ANAO	0.077	-0.050	ENVIRON	0.032	0.016	DTI	0.039	0.041
DVA	-0.054	-0.066	-	-	-	-	-	-
WEATHER	-0.098	-0.050	-	-	-	-	-	-
AEC	-0.005[a]	-0.066	-	-	-	-	-	-
DSS	-0.090	-0.079	-	-	-	-	-	-
ARCHIVES	-0.003[a]	-0.088	-	-	-	-	-	-
INDCOM	-0.097	-0.061	-	-	-	-	-	-
TREASURY	-0.092	-0.033[a]	-	-	-	-	-	-
DPP	0.084	0.079	-	-	-	-	-	-
COMSUPER	-0.109	-0.159	-	-	-	-	-	-
ABS	-0.048	-0.086	-	-	-	-	-	-
CUSTOMS	-0.217	-0.288	-	-	-	-	-	-
ATO	-0.028	-0.052	-	-	-	-	-	-
DEFENCE	-0.103	-0.122	-	-	-	-	-	-
FINANCE	-0.020[a]	-0.047	-	-	-	-	-	-
HEALTH	0.113	0.133	-	-	-	-	-	-
ANCA	-0.058[a]	-0.082	-	-	-	-	-	-
DIR	-0.008[a]	-0.037[a]	-	-	-	-	-	-
DEETYA	-0.032	-0.014[a]	-	-	-	-	-	-
DPIE	-0.037	-0.041	-	-	-	-	-	-
DFAT	-0.095	-0.100	-	-	-	-	-	-

Appendix 6.2 (Contd.)

	Australia			Sweden			UK	
	1990	1996		1993	1996		1990	1996
ADMIN	-0.051	-0.039	-	-	-	-	-	-
DIMA	-0.013 [a]	-0.022	-	-	-	-	-	-
ABARE	-0.071	-0.121	-	-	-	-	-	-
ISC	0.007 [a]	0.039 [a]	-	-	-	-	-	-
COMCARE	0.006 [a]	-0.054	-	-	-	-	-	-
Grades								
SES	0.796	0.896	HIGHCS	0.878	0.920	SENIORCS	1.480	1.562
SO	0.456	0.583	DEPTMAN	0.706	0.772	HIGHCS	1.137	1.206
ASO	0.130	0.190	QUALAD	0.476	0.513	EO	0.509	0.537
OTHER	0.413	0.436	ADMIN	0.264	0.283	ADMIN	0.210	0.232
-	-	-	QUALASST	0.087	0.095	-	-	-

* Note: See Notes to Appendix 6.1.

Appendix 6.3 'Common Specification' Regression Results for Male Civil Servants in 1990/3 and 1996

	Australia			Sweden			UK	
	1990	1996		1993	1996		1990	1996
Constant	7.135	7.205	Constant	8.896	8.888	INTERCEP	5.771	5.868
TENURE	0.029	0.020	TENGOVI	1.3E-3	-3.4E-4 [a]	GOVTEN	0.011	0.016
TENURESQ	-5.9E-4	-3.2E-4	TEN2GOV	1.5E-5	1.5E-5	GOVTENSQ	-1.5E-4	-2.6E-4
AGE	0.025	0.025	AGE	0.026	0.028	AGE	0.027	0.024
AGESQ	-2.8E-4	-2.7E-4	AGESQ	-2.7E-4 [a]	-2.7E-4	AGESQ	-3.2E-4	-2.6E-4
Region								
NSW	-0.119	-0.110	SOUTH	-0.080	-0.098	SCOTLAND	-0.023	-0.006
VIC	-0.112	-0.095	CENTRAL	-0.068	-0.090	NORTH	-0.030	-0.003 [a]
QLD	-0.126	-0.111	NORTH	-0.076	-0.078	YORKHUM	0.015	0.006
SA	-0.108	-0.084	-	-	-	NW	0.020	-0.008
WA	-0.164	-0.101	-	-	-	EMIDLAND	0.058	-0.012
TAS	-0.117	-0.107	-	-	-	WMIDLAND	-0.034	-0.011
NT	-0.077	-0.080	-	-	-	WALES	-0.034	-0.011
-	-	-	-	-	-	EANGLIA	-0.019	-0.025
-	-	-	-	-	-	SW	-0.022	-0.069
-	-	-	-	-	-	NI	0.012 [a]	-0.069
Departments/Agencies								
AIPO	-0.160	-0.116	FORAFF	-0.057	0.008 [a]	MAFF	0.216	0.016
ACCC	-0.049 [a]	-0.076	DEFENCE	0.029	0.074	CABINET	0.164	0.105
PSMPC	-0.047 [a]	-0.128	SOCIALAF	0.012 [a]	0.033	TREASURY	0.155	0.137
AIDAB	-0.057	-0.108	TRANSPRT	-0.036	-0.008 [a]	CUSTOMS	-0.061	0.052
AGPS	-0.113	-0.146	FINANCE	-0.002 [a]	0.018	DEFENSE	-0.404	0.141
ATSIC	0.010 [a]	-0.052	EDUC	-0.032	-1.2E-3 [a]	DFEE	0.081	-0.010
AWM	-0.160	-0.163	AGRI	-0.119	0.022	DOE	0.308	0.166
NCA	0.083	0.077	LABOUR	-0.045	-0.023	HEALTH	0.677	0.108
AGSO	-0.119	-0.030	CULTURE	-0.091	-0.087	HOMEOFF	0.406	0.303
NLA	-0.209	-0.175	TRADE	0.003 [a]	-0.029	COURTS	0.034	0.042
PMC	-0.050	-0.086	PUBAFF	-0.040	-0.018	HERITAGE	0.174	0.140
ANAO	0.013 [a]	-0.072	ENVIRON	-5.4E-4 [a]	-0.059	DTI	0.187	0.117
DVA	-0.073	-0.117	-	-	-	-	-	-
WEATHER	-0.133	-0.121	-	-	-	-	-	-
AEC	-0.024 [a]	-0.072	-	-	-	-	-	-
DSS	-0.107	-0.115	-	-	-	-	-	-
ARCHIVES	-0.097	-0.143	-	-	-	-	-	-
INDCOM	-0.047	-0.058	-	-	-	-	-	-
TREASURY	-0.053	-0.088	-	-	-	-	-	-
DPP	0.147	0.099	-	-	-	-	-	-
COMSUPER	-0.141	-0.178	-	-	-	-	-	-
ABS	-0.097	-0.122	-	-	-	-	-	-
CUSTOMS	-0.276	-0.294	-	-	-	-	-	-
ATO	-0.046	-0.075	-	-	-	-	-	-
DEFENCE	-0.105	-0.106	-	-	-	-	-	-
FINANCE	-0.060	-0.080	-	-	-	-	-	-
HEALTH	0.076	0.062	-	-	-	-	-	-
ANCA	-0.043 [a]	-0.074	-	-	-	-	-	-
DIR	-0.025	-0.072	-	-	-	-	-	-
DEETYA	-0.069	-0.078	-	-	-	-	-	-
DPIE	-0.037	-0.168	-	-	-	-	-	-

Appendix 6.3 (Contd.)

	Australia			Sweden			UK	
	1990	1996		1993	1996		1990	1996
DFAT	-0.122	-0.121	-	-	-	-	-	-
ADMIN	-0.056	-0.068	-	-	-	-	-	-
DIMA	-0.070	-0.089	-	-	-	-	-	-
ABARE	-0.076	-0.119	-	-	-	-	-	-
ISC	-0.028[a]	-0.022[a]	-	-	-	-	-	-
COMCARE	-0.031[a]	-0.088	-	-	-	-	-	-
Grades								
SES	0.669	0.799	HIGHCS	0.898	0.948	SENIORCS	1.369	1.542
SO	0.345	0.479	DEPTMAN	0.730	0.762	HIGHCS	0.853	1.153
ASO	0.092	0.137	QUALAD	0.483	0.524	EO	0.453	0.587
OTHER	0.314	0.374	ADMIN	0.288	0.296	ADMIN	0.297	0.341
			QUALASST	0.124	0.117			

* Note: See Notes to Appendix 6.1.

Index

For Product Safety Concerns and Information please contact our EU
representative GPSR@taylorandfrancis.com Taylor & Francis Verlag GmbH,
Kaufingerstraße 24, 80331 München, Germany

Printed and bound by CPI Group (UK) Ltd, Croydon, CR0 4YY
08/05/2025
01864366-0011